Published by Matronita Press

Canada House, Morasha, Jerusalem, Israel

To contact Matronita Press directly, email our Customer Care Department at: www.matronitapress.com

Levy, Rivka
      Talk to God and Fix Your Life / Rivka Levy – Second edition

ISBN: Trade Paperback,   **978-965-7739-08-2**

SECOND EDITION

Printed in the USA

"*Joy is the remedy for everything*"

- Rebbe Nachman of Breslev

The Happy Workshop

An eight week journey to real, lasting happiness

Rivka Levy

Contents

Introduction: Why I wrote the Happy Workshop

When I was growing up, I was always told that there are two types of people: 'happy-go-lucky' types, and 'serious-depressed' types. Or to put it another way, the only people who could be really happy were the ones that didn't really think about anything too much, and who certainly didn't waste their time pondering 'the meaning of life' and other deep rubbish like that.

There was just one problem: I'm a 'serious-depressed' sort of person, who really, really wanted to be happy. So for quite a few years, I got very stuck trying to square that circle.

For a while, I became a workaholic, and I was kind of happy when I was frantically rushing to meet a ridiculous deadline, or rushing to pick my kids up from their daycare, or rushing to gulp down a sandwich for lunch so that I could get back to work – because I simply didn't have time to think about the 'big' questions, like: 'What's it all for?'

But then, my business failed. Well, it didn't so much fail as jumped off a very big cliff, and I went from earning five figures a month to less than the national wage. In the space of a few months, I had four very big challenges to my happiness:

- I went from being financially comfortable, to losing my home because I couldn't afford the mortgage repayments

- I went from being a successful 'high flier' to being a depressed, unemployed, nervous wreck

- The financial problems we were having put a lot of pressure on my marriage, and I started to have massive rows with my husband because of all the stress

- As our debts mounted, we kept moving community every couple of years, in order to live more cheaply – which left me and my family with a sense of being permanently 'dislocated'

All of a sudden, I couldn't 'work myself happy'; or 'shop myself happy'; or 'vacation myself happy' – which is when I had a really amazing realization: even when I had my business, and my fat bank account, and my home, and my luxuries – even *then*, I hadn't been really, genuinely happy.

All that was happening is that my life had been so full of distractions, I hadn't noticed how miserable I was.

Once I realized that, I started searching for the path to real happiness. Not the temporary, fake 'happy' that we feel when we get a promotion, or a new car, or a new designer handbag, or when our team 'wins big'. I was after the real deal. I was after a 'happy' that would stay with me even if I didn't have a lot of money; even if none of my dreams were coming true, even if I was going through an incredibly hard time.
My search for 'real happy' took me to massive seminars involving hundreds of participants; it took me to Neuro-Linguistic Programmers, who spent hours trying to get me to 'visualise' what my happy would look like; it took me through three shrinks, two countries, and one absolutely massive personal crisis.

But amazingly enough, in the end, I found it.

I didn't find it in all the tapping and visualisation; I didn't find it in all the 'clever' psychobabble or self-help books; I didn't even find it on the therapist's couch, although I spent a couple of years and a fortune of money to learn that it wasn't really there, either.

In the end, I found it in the writings of a Rabbi who lived 200 years' ago, and who made it his life's work to teach people how to really be happy. I'd been through so many other things, that initially, I was very sceptical that Rabbi Nachman of Breslev's teachings were going to be anything more than a band-aid, or a temporary solution that would wear off, or wear through, as quickly as all the other stuff had.

But it didn't.

Five years' on, I'm happier than I've ever been, and not because my life is perfect. I still have so many things that are not exactly how I'd dreamed they'd be: I still have a massive overdraft and struggle to meet my mortgage payments; I still don't have a job; I haven't bought a new pair of shoes in a couple of years – but I'm happy, and most days, I wake up with a smile on my face.

Rabbi Nachman really knew the secret of happiness, and now, I want to share that secret with you.

This book is not a 'theoretical discussion' that sounds good on paper but just doesn't work in practise. It's a practical guide for real people who don't have 'perfect' lives, but who still really want to be happy

If you follow the guidelines in the Happy Workshop, keep an open mind, and do the exercises to the best of your ability, I guarantee that at the end of eight weeks, you'll feel happier and more content with life.

And the more you make the 'Happy Workshop' principles part of your life, the more you'll see lasting, fundamental, positive changes in how you manage the ups and downs that all of us have to deal with.

It's a great thing to be genuinely happy with your life, and by the time you've finished reading this book, you'll have taken a quantum leap closer to attaining it.

Week 1 – Real Happy

A little while ago, my husband and I arranged a weekend away together, without the kids, at what was meant to be an uplifting retreat in a gorgeous part of the country. The main speaker at the retreat was someone that my husband and I know and love, and we were really psyched up about how amazing the weekend was going to be.

- It was going to be romantic time for us to catch up with each other.

- We were going to recharge our spiritual batteries, from all the amazing lectures.

- We were going to meet some amazing people who were on the same wavelength, and hopefully forge some new friendships.

Except, none of those things happened.

I got to the 'romantic' retreat only to find that my husband had been misinformed, and that everyone else had brought their kids with them. What's more, the lecture hall (which was also doubling up as the canteen) had been arranged so that the women and the loud, screaming kids were on one side, and the men were on the other.

I didn't know anyone else there, and it was really hard to break the ice because all the other women were busy feeding and entertaining their kids.

I couldn't hear what the guest speaker was saying, as the noise from my side of the hall was deafening, and he speaks pretty quietly.

The food was nice enough, but I'd been seated next to an apparently ravenous woman who was taking everything off the communal serving plates before they got to me. She wasn't a big salad or rice fan, so that – and a bit of leftover gravy – is pretty much what I ate.

Yes, I could have gone looking for more food elsewhere, but I was already starting to feel a bit demoralised, and I just couldn't be bothered making the effort. As the evening wore on, I was really starting to resent the famished lady, and her triple helpings of food.

The last straw was that I barely saw my husband all night. He was having a great time, making new friends, discussing deep ideas and listening to the lectures.

He was enjoying himself so much that I didn't have the heart to interrupt him to come for a 'romantic' walk with his increasingly moody wife. So instead, I went to bed.

The next morning, I tried again – but it was another helping of the same noise, loneliness and social discomfort. So I gave up, and decided to go for my 'romantic' walk by myself, and to talk to my 'Higher Power' about it all.

(We'll learn more about talking to our 'Higher Power' a bit later on...)

For the first time in ages, I was starting to feel really miserable, and I was trying to work out why, exactly. While I was walking and talking, I started to get some insight in to why I was feeling so down:

1. I had very **inflated expectations** of what the Retreat was going to be, and what it was going to do – and they hadn't been met

2. I was being **very judgemental** of the other people at the Retreat – particularly the chubby woman sitting next to me who ate like a horse.

It took me a while to think it all through, but once I realized I'm not owed anything, and that it was my own judgements and expectations that were weighing me down so much, I felt much better.

I went back for the afternoon session, and this time, I actually got to hear every word of what the lecturer was saying, as they'd given the kids a different room to play in.

It was all about….happiness.

The lecturer was explaining that if a person didn't have genuine happiness, they didn't have anything. If they weren't genuinely happy, even the good things they had in their life wouldn't register with them.

They wouldn't care that they had a roof over their heads, or that they could breathe, and see, and walk around unaided, or that they had people who loved them, or food on the table, or nice furniture, or a great job - none of it would even matter to a miserable person.

Until it disappeared.

Then, they'd realize what they'd had, and what they hadn't appreciated – and they'd start to feel even more miserable.

At this point, a lot of the people in the room started to fidget, because we'd all just recognized ourselves. Someone raised their hand, and asked the question that we'd all been dying to ask:

How do we really get happy?

The answer was simple: appreciate what you have.

Appreciate that your body works, and that you don't need to spend hours having kidney dialysis, or waiting for your name to come to the top of a very long lung-transplant list.

Appreciate that you have parents who love and care for you, even if they aren't very good at showing it.

Appreciate every breath you take. There is no guarantee that you'll be here tomorrow. Every single day we have is a privilege, a gift. We have to learn to appreciate these amazing privileges we have, because if we don't recognize that the mere fact of being alive is a gift, we can never by truly happy.

We were all blown away. It was so quiet in the room, you could have heard a pin drop. For me, it was the first time in my life that I'd heard a proper answer to the question of 'how can we really be happy?'

Every other answer I'd ever heard or read was conditional, like:

- You'll be happy if you exercise more
- You'll be happy if you eat better
- You'll be happy if you lose 50 pounds
- You'll be happy if make more than you'll spend
- You'll be happy once you find Mr / Ms Right
- You'll be happy once you switch jobs
- You'll be happy once you start a family
- You'll be happy once you move apartment

But what if you just can't find the time to jog for an hour a day? Or the diet just isn't getting anywhere fast, even though you've stuck to it for months? Or you've dated everyone in the whole universe, and nothing ever worked out?

Then what?

If you are like 99.9% of humanity, you get miserable.

But the answer I heard at the Retreat worked for everyone, and across all circumstances. The answer was not to change your circumstances – most of us would already be doing that, if we could.

The answer was to **be happy with whatever your circumstances happen to be, and to look for all the good you already have in your life, however small.**

Happy Workshop Principle 1:

Don't make your happiness depend on an external change in your circumstances. What if it never changes?
Instead, be happy with whatever your circumstances are, and look for all the good you already have in your life, however small.

What????

How can I be happy, if my life isn't going how I planned? How can I be happy if I'm out of work, or don't have enough money to pay for a vacation, or I'm 43 and still single, or I'm 43 and having terrible fights with my spouse, or my kid is flunking out of school, or I hate my job, or I hate my neighbourhood but can't afford to move....

All of this sounds like a fair argument, until we remember that *if we could change these things, we would.*

If you can change the circumstances that are making you miserable, go right ahead.
But if you can't?

If even, despite your best efforts, you are still sliding into more debt at the end of the month; or still not married, or still not solving your 'problem', whatever your problem might be – are you going to be miserable for the rest of your life?

'Happy' doesn't just happen to a person. You have to fight for 'happy'. You have to commit to 'happy'. You have to search for 'happy' in even the saddest places. Which brings us to our first set of Happy Workshop exercises:

[You'll need a few sheets of paper at least as big as A4, plus coloured pens or coloured pencils for the exercises in this book.]

Before we start Exercise 1, take a few minutes to think about what makes you happy.

The answer is different for everyone, but the more you can try to capture your idea of 'happy', the easier it will be for you understand what is really going on in your subconscious mind, and what's being triggered when you start to feel 'un'happy.

What makes us happy?

- A good meal
- Appreciation (from the boss, from our spouse)
- A warm bed

- A good book
- Skiing a 'Black' run
- Being at home
- Being away
- A smile from our child
- Enough money (for what?)
- A deep conversation with a friend
- Being needed
- Getting attention

These are just some ideas to get you started. Take your time, and try to put as many things on your list as you can. It will help you to refer back to it as you work your way through the rest of the Happy Workshop.

Exercise 1: What makes us happy?

Write your name in the centre of your sheet of paper, and put a box or circle around it. Draw a line off called 'happy' and at the end of that line, list everything that makes you happy.

(Be honest – if watching a beautiful sunset doesn't really make you happy, don't put it on your list just because you think you should. By the same token, if you love to smoke, then make sure you put 'smoking a cigarette' down on your list, even though it's not very politically correct.)

You can put things on your list that you already have, and that you don't yet have, but that you think you would like.

When that's done…

You can either stop here and mull over your happy list for a bit, or you can carry on to Exercise 2.

Before you do, take a few minutes to think about what makes you sad, or 'un'happy?

Exercise 2: What makes us sad?

If you have space on the same sheet of paper you used for Exercise 1, draw another line off from your 'name box' or 'name circle', and call it 'sad'. Now, write down everything that makes you sad, or 'un'happy.

(Again, be honest. If it makes you sad when you get angry with your child, write that down. If it makes you sad that you aren't a millionaire, or that you aren't 18 any more, or that you aren't a pop star, put it down – the more things you capture on your list and the more honest you are, the easier it will be to reach 'real happiness' by the end of the Happy Workshop.)

If you want, you can stop here for now, and spend a bit of time letting Exercises 1 and 2 sink in before continuing.

Exercise 3:

Go back to your 'happy' list from Exercise 1. Go through the list, and see how many of the things that you said make you happy, you already have. Put a star next to those things.

- Do you have clean air to breathe?
- Can you have a hot shower whenever you want?
- Did someone care enough about you to give you this book?

Start trying to think about the small things that make us happy, not just the 'big' things, like a lottery win or a luxury cruise. If your happy list only has 'big' things on it, go back and do it again, and try to include all the small happinesses you have every day, like central heating, or air conditioning, or a pair of comfortable shoes that don't rub your heels, or a good friend, or a great cup of coffee.

The more you notice and recognize these 'small happinesses' the happier and more content you will feel.

(We'll cover this in more detail a bit later on.)

The Happy Workshop Definition of 'Real' Happy

A drug addict will define 'happy' as their next hit. A womanizer will define 'happy' as their next sexual conquest. A chocoholic will define 'happy' as a KitKat or Snickers bar – but none of these definitions are the 'real' happy.

Happy Workshop Principle 2:

Real happy doesn't come from externals. Real happy stays with you, even when things aren't going your way.

So many people, even when life is great, still aren't happy, because they are constantly focusing on what they don't have, or constantly worrying about what tomorrow will bring.

I was certainly that way, even when I was outwardly living a very successful life running my own communications business.

I had a great, interesting, well-paid, 'prestigious' job, ghost-writing speeches and articles for a bunch of Government ministers.

I had a great husband, who put up with my crazy deadlines and even brought me cups of tea when I was still bashing away at the keyboard in the wee hours.

I had two beautiful, healthy daughters, who I was so grateful to have in my life, as we'd been trying to have kids for a few years before they came along.

I had a nice house, that was very nicely renovated and furnished; I had quite a lot of 'spare' cash, and I could buy whatever clothes I wanted, whenever I wanted; I was thin! I was healthy! I had great hair!

But the smallest little setbacks still made me miserable.

If I felt I wasn't getting enough appreciation from my boss, I could sulk and feel depressed for days. If my kid came home from the nursery with a note saying she had nits, I was devastated, and would go into panic mode trying to kill them off. If one of my houseplants died, I'd mope around for an hour and feel like life was really unfair, and that 'bad things' always happened to me.

I had happy moments, like when I won a particularly lucrative contract for work, or when I was on holiday or having a meal out, but with hindsight, I could never really enjoy those high spots, because I always had one eye looking out for the next curve ball.

I never 'lived in the moment', which meant that I missed a lot of chances to appreciate all the good that I had. Even in the middle of the expensive meal out, or the family trip to the seaside, I'd be worrying about meeting my clients' deadlines the next day, or planning the next move to try to expand my business.

Happy Workshop Principle 3:

Live in the moment. Don't worry about tomorrow until you are there.

Exercise 4: Top ten 'happy' priorities

Look at your happy list. Pick out the top 10 things that make you happy, and prioritise them from one to 10, one being the most important priority.

Once you have got your prioritised Top Ten list of things that make you happy, write it down on a separate piece of paper. Write next to each priority how much time you spend on it, on average, in a week.

(Guesstimates are fine, but again, be honest! If you write down 'kids' as your first priority and 'gardening' as priority number 8, don't just assume you spend more time with your kids than with your cucumbers. Go through the last week, and write down the most accurate figures you can for how much time you are giving each priority on your list.)

We'll finish this first week with some interesting questions, that you can mull over before you move on to Week 2:

Does your list of priorities accurately reflect the time you are spending on them?

If 'no', why not?

Are you spending enough time on your higher, 'happy-making' priorities, or is your time getting siphoned-off into lower priorities, or even, into things that aren't on your priority list?

What can you do to spend more of your time doing the things that make you really happy?

Week 2 - Great Expectations

A few years' ago, one of the big supermarket chains in the UK ran an advertising campaign to encourage consumers to 'be more demanding'. The idea was that instead of settling for second rate service and slow delivery and less-than-perfect fruit, consumers should pay a bit more and be more demanding about what they were getting in return.

I often think about that ad, because it sums up a lot of our modern expectations about life – and it's the perfect recipe for stress, disappointment and sadness.

Part of the problem is that everywhere we go, we are being told that things are 100% in human control, and it's all down to us.

So when our train is late because of 'leaves on the line'; or because someone pulled the emergency stop and it backed everything up for half an hour while the station police tried to sort it all out; or simply because the driver left a little later than he should have, and it's been one of those days – instead of calmly and serenely accepting that life really isn't in our control, and we are going to be late today, we get cross. We get furious. We get vengeful. We start to blame everything and everyone around us that things aren't going 100% to plan – including ourselves.

- "Why didn't I wake up earlier?"
- "Why did it take the kids so long to eat breakfast today?"
- "Why couldn't I have found a better parking spot?"
- "Why was there so much traffic?"
- "Why is the train service so poor?"

The list goes on and on.

When we start to 'be more demanding', and to demand that everything goes 100% how we'd like it to, we forget about a vital, crucial point: life is not in our control. Not even the relatively 'small' things like getting to work on time, or getting a perfectly ripe pear delivered to our front door. And if we can't control the small things, we certainly can't control the big things in life.

Happy Workshop Principle 4:

We can't control everything that happens to us, and neither can anyone else.

Ego Attack...

Most of us don't like to hear that our life isn't 100% in our control. Most of us like to think that there are 'rules' for how life works, and that if we follow the rules, and work hard, and try, and try some more, sooner or later, we'll get what we want, and life will go the way we want it to.

Everyone thinks like that until they discover the hard way that it's simply not true.
I certainly used to think like that. When I was a high-flying businesswoman, I used to believe that all my success and financial security was down to my own hard work.

I used to work through the night to meet my clients' (unreasonable...) deadlines; I used to go over things four and even five times before I sent them off, to make sure they were 'perfect'; I used to have extremely high standards for my employees, and I wouldn't tolerate even minor mistakes or imperfections.

Today, I cringe to think about how exacting, how mean, how arrogant I was with the people who were helping me in the business.

I was one, massive, ego on legs, and not only in the workplace.

If my kids took longer than five minutes to get ready to go out, I'd have a massive tantrum about how long they were making we wait. If my husband didn't manage to pick out exactly the piece of jewellery I wanted for my birthday, I'd be terribly depressed and sulk for weeks. If a friend didn't call me enough, or sympathise with me enough, or invite me round enough, I'd either be in the pit of despair about how unlikeable I was, or blaming them for not being very nice people.

I hated having to wait in line in the supermarket, or having to queue when I was picking up a sandwich for lunch – what a waste of my valuable time! I hated having to let people go in front of me when I was driving – clearly, whatever I had to do was far more important than whatever they were busy with. I hated having to give in, or having to do things someone else's way, or having to take other people's opinions or feelings into account.

In short, I was a horrible spoilt brat. I was terribly demanding. And I was also horribly, terribly miserable.

Negative emotions

This week, we are going to start to work on some of the negative emotions that are preventing us from being happy. All too often, we look at negative emotions in a very superficial way, and tell ourselves that we are miserable because we don't have 'X', or because we don't have 'Y'.

We're not going to do that in the Happy Workshop. We're going to dig deep, and start tracing our negative emotions back to their source. If this sounds like hard work – you're right! It is. But there are no quick fixes when it comes to really finding true, lasting happiness.

If we don't do the work, and if we don't dig our negative emotions out at their roots, they will just pop again in a few weeks' time, or in a few months' time, except with a different name.

This happens all the time with people who are in therapy. They spend years and years talking about all the terrible things their parents did or didn't do; and all the expectations they had for life that were never fulfilled; and about all the problems and issues and hardships they have – without ever getting to a place where they feel genuinely happy and fulfilled.

Why?

Because most therapy and nearly all therapists only deal with the symptoms, not the root.

Remember our Happy Workshop Principle number 2:

Happy Workshop Principle 2:

Real happy doesn't come from externals. Real happy stays with you, even when things aren't going your way.

With that in mind, let's do some digging, and start to uncover what is *really* making you miserable.

How do we know when we really aren't 'happy'?

In the modern world, there is such a big stigma attached to being 'sad' that a lot of us go through life convinced we're not 'sad'. But feeling sad isn't the only clue that we aren't feeling genuine happiness.

There are a whole bunch of other, more socially-acceptable, negative emotions that are a clear warning signal that we aren't really happy.

Here's a partial list, to get you started:

- Fear
- Anger
- Worry
- Stress – (a great one that a lot of people hide behind)
- Hatred
- Jealousy

Exercise 5: Negative emotions

Take a sheet of paper, and write on the top: 'My negative emotions'. Take a few minutes, and using the above list as a guide, try to write down whatever negative emotions you are currently experiencing in your life.

If you are having trouble capturing them, think back to the conversations you have with your close friends or family members, and write down your catchphrases.

Some people will talk a lot about how situation x is 'stressing them out' – which is a very common disguise for a negative emotion.

Someone else will talk about how they feel really angry; or frustrated; yet another person will talk about how they are 'worrying about something'; someone else will say that 'they hate when... [fill in the blank].'

Whenever you hear yourself saying a catch-phrase like: 'I'm stressed', what you are really saying is: 'I'm unhappy'.

When you have finished your list, either get a new sheet of paper, or turn the paper over.

Now, pick your main 'negative emotion' and write down everything that you can think of that is currently 'stressing you out' or making you angry, or that you are worrying about.

Don't hold anything back; remember, the more honest you can be in these mind map exercises, the easier it will be for you ultimately to work out what is really making you miserable, and how to really fix it.

When you've completed your list of triggers for negative emotions, rank them from 1 up, 1 being the thing that most stresses you out; or most worries you; or most makes you upset or sad.

You can either stop here for a bit to let the last exercise sink in, or continue.

Spiritual mechanics

Now, we are ready to introduce another key Happy Workshop principle:

Happy Workshop Principle 5:

One of the key reasons we feel sad and depressed is because we have expectations that aren't being met.

Great expectations

From the time we are born, all of us are dealing with a whole bunch of expectations of how our life is going to be (usually, based on a Disney movie…). These expectations start very young, and they are present at every stage of our lives.

From the time 'Junior' is born, his parents are already comparing him to all the neighbours' kids, to see whose baby is sitting up first; talking first; crawling first. If Junior isn't sleeping through the night by three months, their stress levels are already starting to rise, and they are increasingly worried that they must be doing something 'wrong'.

If Junior doesn't sit up right on the six month mark, his parents start to panic that he has some sort of undiagnosed developmental problem; if Junior isn't saying his first words by 12 months, the parents feel so guilty that they haven't been reading Charles Dickens novels to him every night and buying the baby flashcards.

Then, we get to kindergarten stage, and the pressure, stress, blame and anxiety goes up a whole other level: Junior isn't reading at the age of three! Which means Junior won't get into a good primary school! Which means he won't get into a good high school! Which means he won't have good teachers and will flunk the subjects he needs to get into a good university! If Junior doesn't have a 'First' from a prestigious university, no-one is even going to employ him as a tea boy in this competitive economy; he won't make enough money to live on, he'll never be a success, he'll never move out or get married – and he'll be a depressing, miserable failure for the rest of his life.

Junior is three years' old.

But even if we have normal, healthy, minimal expectations for our children, we still have a massively long list of expectations about how our own lives should be:

All of us have expectations about:

- How we should look (thin and beautiful);
- How we should eat (healthy and nutritious; or sumptuous and gourmet)
- Where we should live (a big, beautiful house in the 'right' neighbourhood)
- Who we should spend the rest of our lives with, and when, and how (the 'perfect wedding'…)
- How many kids we should have, and how they should behave, and how we should feel about them
- How our spouse should be (they should always give in to our every whim, and not expect us to change or do anything too much like hard work)
- How our parents should be (they should pay for everything and always put us first, even after we've left home)
- How our homes, schools, work places, neighbours and friends should be
- How we should be (and if you are like most people, this list is the biggest, most onerous, and most depressing one of the lot)

Exercise 6: The great expectation trap

Take a look at your 'happy list' mind map from Exercise 1 last week, and your list of 'negative emotion' triggers that you wrote down this week, in Exercise 5.

First, look at how many of the things that make you feel sad, stressed, angry - or whatever your main negative emotion is – make you feel bad because you have some sort of expectation that isn't being met, and underline them.

Then, look at your 'happy' list from Exercise 1 – and underline everything that is based on an expectation being met.

When you are done, you can stop and pause for thought, or continue on to the next section.

The pursuit of happiness

One of the foundations of Western society is 'life, liberty and the pursuit of happiness'. The Founding Fathers built a whole country around those principles, and today, American culture is so pervasive that these principles have been firmly hardwired in to nearly every single one of us.

As a result, so many of us spend so much of our lives trying to 'pursue' happiness, as though it's some sort of external thing you have to pin down and trap.

All the ads we see, and all the TV programs we are addicted to, and all the movies we watch all help to reinforce the idea that if we buy *that* brand of jeans, we'll be happy; or if we drink *that* sort of cola, we'll be happy; or if we look like *that* actor; and live in *that* neighbourhood, and have *that many* zeros in our bank balance, we'll be happy.

But if that's really true, why are so many of the world's successful, rich, beautiful, famous people so miserable, messed-up and depressed? Why do so many of them have drink or drug addictions? Why do so many of them have such big problems staying married? Why do so many of them kill themselves, or live a lifestyle that's almost a guarantee for them dying young?

If they are doing all the things that are meant to make us all happy, why are they still so miserable?

The answer is that **real happiness is internal.**

If you really want to be happy, you have to learn how to be happy with your lot in life.

So now, you may have a very good question to ask:

How can we be happy with our lot (ie, really happy) if we have a whole bunch of expectations that aren't being met?

The answer is our Happy Workshop Principle 6:

Happy Workshop Principle 6:

The fewer expectations we have, the happier we will be.

We all have choices to make in life. We can choose to 'be more demanding', and have an ever-expanding list of things that we 'expect' from ourselves, from other people and from life generally.

But we have to realize that the more things we expect, the more likely it is that our expectations won't all be met.

And when our expectations don't get met, we feel miserable.

If we choose to expect less, we're making it much easier for expectations to be met, and even, to be exceeded – and that's guaranteed to put a smile on anyone's face.

Exercise 7: Our underlying expectations

Go back over your 'happy' list from Exercise 1, and start to pull out the underlying expectations.

Take a new sheet of paper, and write down what you are really expecting from:

- Your spouse?
- Your kids?
- Your parents and siblings?
- Your friends?
- Your acquaintances?
- Your work?
- Your boss?
- Your education?
- Yourself?

Tip: you can usually catch an expectation with the word 'should'. Eg:

- I *should* make my family eat healthy food
- I *should* go to bed at a good time
- My house *should* be tidier
- My kids *should* behave better
- My husband *should* give me more attention
- My parents *should* offer to help more

- I *should* be able to afford to go abroad on vacation at least twice a week
- I *should* get a promotion

Exercise 8: What happens when your expectations aren't met?

Look at your list of expectations from Exercise 7. How do you feel when your expectations aren't being met?

(Again, be as honest as you can – this list is for you, not anyone else! Don't worry about writing things that will make you look good, or giving the 'right' answers. The more honest you are about how you really feel, the faster you'll find a lasting solution to the issues that are really making you miserable.)

That's it for this week. Over the next few days, try to catch the things you are expecting from yourself, the people in your life and your situations. Notice how you feel when things are 'going your way' and an expectation has been met, and how you feel when things aren't going the way you'd like them to.

Week 3 – Catching conflicting priorities

Catch 22

When I was growing up in the Eighties, 'Women's Lib' was really starting to hit the headlines in a big way. Every week, there'd be another story about 'the first female this', or 'the first female that' in the country. My teachers (usually the lady ones) would bring the newspaper clipping in, and there'd be an excited discussion about how 'women could do anything they wanted to, these days'.

It all sounded so amazing, so perfect, so wonderful. But my mum wasn't so convinced. My mum was working a full-time job because she had to, and was also trying to balance that with raising a large family of five kids.

"I think Women's Lib is a con," she told me. "All it means is that you get stuck working on top of having to do everything else that women still have to do to keep the home going."

I think I was 12 when we had this conversation, so at the time it didn't really register as one of the great truths of our time.

But when I hit 30, and I had two small kids and a hectic career running my own business – my mum's words really came back to haunt me. Because whatever I tried to do to balance my home life and my job, I felt I was always caught in a Catch 22 situation.

All too often, I'd have some ridiculous deadline to meet, and it would clash with a birthday party I'd said they could go to; or with a promise I'd made to take them out for an ice-cream, or with a plan to take them to the park or do a picnic in the back garden.

And it didn't just happen once or twice, it was happening all the time.

My kids were getting increasingly sullen, sulky and attention-seeking, because even when I made the decision to be 'with them' – I was only with them in body. My mind was off working through my latest speech or article, or I was preoccupied trying *not* to think about work, or to stress about it, and failing miserably.

I tried buying them tons of books and toys to keep them happy and keep my guilt-feelings at bay. I tried finding 'educational' activities they could do on the computer, or 'educational' videos (like Shrek…) for them to watch for an hour or two to buy myself more time to get whatever I was working on finished.

But deep down, I knew it was a cop-out. I also knew that sooner or later, something would have to give because I had two conflicting priorities in my life that simply couldn't occupy the same space.

It took ages for me to choose between my job and my family. I literally spent years of my life pinging backwards and forwards between quitting and not quitting, torn between the money and status that my work was giving me and the fact that I was really not being the sort of mum I wanted to be for my kids, and the sort of wife I wanted to be for my husband.

In the end, the family won out, but until my conflicting priorities got resolved, I was terribly unhappy about it all. I spent a lot of my time in a very negative mindset, constantly:

- Complaining
- Feeling dissatisfied about my life
- Trying to get things 'back on track', or 'back in balance'
- Expending a lot of effort to 'fix' a problem that there was no quick fix for
- Blaming other people (especially my children, and occasionally my clients)
- Blaming myself (that I couldn't work faster, delegate more, sleep less)
- Getting frustrated that whatever I tried to do, I always felt someone, somewhere was losing out.

Finding the root cause

For years and years, I was trying this 'quick fix' and that 'quick fix' to try and sort the problem out. I tried live-in help, live-out help, full-time day care and part-time school. I tried flexi-working, part-time working, working from home, working for myself – but nothing really helped for very long, because I wasn't dealing with the root cause of the problem.

The root cause of the problem is that I am a perfectionist, and that whatever I'm doing, I have to do it 100%.

For as long as I was working, even a little bit, even part-time, the job took over my life, and left me no 'headspace' for my family.

My kids were feeling increasingly neglected, and started to play up and 'act out' even when I was spending more time with them, because they could feel that I wasn't really 'with them'.

The same thing was also happening in my marriage. Yes, me and my husband would go out for expensive meals out, and we'd schedule 'date nights' and weekends away, but it was all a sticking plaster over a massively painful issue: my work was my main priority, and it was always winning out over my family commitments.

Until the conflict between my home and my job was properly addressed and resolved, I simply couldn't be genuinely happy.

Until I faced up to the real problem, I was just going round and round in circles, trying to do the impossible and figure out new ways of making my two big conflicting priorities agree.

Happy Workshop Principle 7:

We will only find genuine happiness once we figure out why we're REALLY unhappy.

Catching the real culprit

While I was in the middle of it all, it was very hard for me to admit what the real problem was that was making me unhappy, so instead, I tried to divert the blame onto other people, or places.

- It was the school's fault that my daughter was so difficult...
- It was my client's fault that I had to work through the night again instead of going out with my husband...
- It was Maggie Thatcher, (the first British female Prime Minister), and all the expectations she'd set up for women and their careers!

Working out what was really at the bottom of it all was really hard, because honestly, I didn't want to know. I wasn't ready to face it or deal with it, which is why it literally took me years.

Most people have a vested interest in NOT catching the real culprit or 'hot button issue' that's really making them unhappy. Why? Because trying to resolve two massively conflicting priorities often requires some big, and potentially very scary, changes to be made.

People are resistant to change, even the changes that are truly going to make them happy.

So before we start the next set of exercises, take a few minutes to have an honest conversation with yourself: do you really want to get to the bottom of why your life is so stressful, hectic and miserable? Or do you want a 'quick fix' that will make you feel good for about five minutes that you are 'doing something useful' – but really won't change anything?

If you are still at the stage of wanting the 'quick fix', you can either do the next set of exercises anyway (but be aware that your vested interest is skewing the results) or skip them and come back when you're ready to face the truth.

If you're ready to get to the bottom of what's really making you miserable, you can do it in a week, by going through the following mind map exercises.

Exercise 9 – Catching our conflicting priorities

In Exercise 4, I asked you to make a list of things that make you happy, and to prioritise it, ranking the things in order of how important they are to you. I then asked you to go back and write next to each priority the amount of time you are really spending on it.

In Exercise 5, I asked you to make a list of the main things that are triggering your negative emotions, and making you feel unhappy, stressed, worried or anxious. We also asked you to rank your negative emotion triggers, with '1' being the thing that most stresses you out etc, all the way down the list.

Now, in Exercise 9, we are going to use these two lists to try to catch your conflicting priorities, and get an accurate picture of what's really making you unhappy.

Look at your 'happy' priorities:

- Does the amount of time you are spending on each one accurately reflect its ranking? As a general rule, the more time you spend on something, the more important it is to you.

- If the time you are spending on any 'priority' and the ranking you've given it don't match up, that is a clue that **your priority list is not a truthful reflection of your life.** Remember, the more time you spend on something, the more of a **real** priority it is.

- Take a different coloured pen, and star the priorities that don't match up. This is where our work is going to begin today.

Example:

I wrote down on my happy priorities list that my spouse is my main priority. I put my friends, as my third or even fourth priority. On an average day, I spend over an hour talking to my friends; calling them, SMSing them, Skyping them or even, popping round for a chat. I spend less than half an hour a day talking to my spouse (sitting watching TV next to them doesn't count...)

Clearly, my priorities don't add up. My **real priority** is my friends, not my spouse.

Once you've caught any 'mismatched' priorities, write them down on a new, separate piece of paper.

If you don't have any 'mismatched priorities', lucky you! It means that your stated priorities are real, and accurately reflecting the way you live your life. You can skip Exercise 10, and go on to Exercise 11.

Exercise 10 – Making our priorities 'match up'

Most of us have at least one 'mismatched priority', where we'd really like to be spending more time on a particular thing, person or area, (or at least, that's what we are telling ourselves.)

This next exercise is going to help us try to clarify what's really going on, and is going to help us catch the 'real culprit' that's really making us miserable.

Go back to your prioritised 'happy' list from Exercise 4. Rewrite your list according to the time you **actually** spend on each activity or item. Write your list in descending order, with the priority that's taking the most time (on average) at the top.

Now, take a different coloured pen. Read through your list, and star the priorities you would like to change.

Once you're done, take two other different coloured pens. If you would like to spend more time on a particular priority, write an 'up' arrow ↑ next to it. If you would like to spend less time on a particular priority, write a 'down' arrow ↓ next to it. If you are happy with the amount of time you are spending on a particular priority, don't write anything next to it.

Example

I wrote down 'exercise' as something that made me happy, and ranked it as number 3 on my happy list. However, I spend on average less than five minutes a day exercising. I really would like to spend more time in the gym working out, playing tennis or going for a walk, so I'm going to put a ↑ next to it.
I wrote down 'work' as something that made me happy, but I only ranked it as number 6. I currently spend 10 hours a day at work, on average. I'd like to spend less time in the office, and more time doing things that **really** make me happier. So I'm going to put a ↓ next to it.

When you are done, take a clean sheet of paper, and make two columns on it. Call column one: 'Things I'd like to spend more time doing'. Call column two: 'Things I'd like to spend less time doing'.

You will probably want to refer back to these exercises again in the future, so keep them in a safe place. In the meantime, start to think about how you can make more time for the gym, and spend less time at work.

Don't worry! As the Happy Workbook continues, we will give you the tools to find real, lasting answers to solving these conflicting priorities. For now, it's enough just to have an honest picture of your life, and to start to see what fundamental issues may be making you unhappy.

Exercise 11 – What's really making me miserable?

Go back to your 'negative emotions' triggers from Exercise 5, and make sure you have your prioritised list from Exercise 4 in front of you as well.

Now, we are going to try and catch some of the conflicting priorities that are causing us stress, anxiety and worry.

The easiest way to do this is to talk you through some examples:

Example:

I have 'a messy house' as a number 4 on my 'sad' or 'upset' or 'angry' list. I have 'happy, well-adjusted kids' as a number 2 on my 'happy' list.

How often do I get angry with the kids, or upset and frustrated with them, because of all the mess they make?

Are 'happy kids' really a bigger priority to me than 'clean house'? If yes, then I need to do some work to have my behaviour reflect what my **real priority** is.

Example:

I have 'financial security' as a number 4 on my 'happy' list. I have 'replacing my old kitchen' as a number 6 on my list of things that are making me miserable. I'm planning to take out a big loan to renovate my kitchen, which I'm going to struggle to repay every month.

Is replacing my old kitchen really more important than having more financial peace of mind? Will going into more debt really make me happy, or will I just end up more stressed every month when I have to meet the repayments?

Example:

I put 'being with someone I love' as number 1 on my 'happy' list. I put 'being pressured to commit to a relationship' as number 4 on my list of things that are stressing me out.

Which one is really more important to me? If I keep backing away from committing to a relationship, then how am I going to achieve my main goal of 'being with someone I love'?

NB: The point is not to try and find answers or resolutions for these issues or conflicts. We'll discuss that side of things more a bit later. For now, we're just trying to catch the conflicts and contradictions that we all have in our lives, to build an accurate picture of what is really making us miserable.

You can stop there, if you want, and let it all sink in.

If you want more food for thought, here are a few questions that may help shed some light on finding some possible solutions to these issues and dilemmas in the future?

- What are my limits, or boundaries? Are they reasonable?
- Am I being consistent?
- What expectations to I have of myself and other people (go back to Exercise 7, if you need a reminder)
- Are they reasonable?
- Do I expect the same from myself as I expect from others? Why / why not?
- What am I prepared to let go of?

- What can I do to forge a 'happy' compromise between my expectations?
- If I have two conflicting priorities, which one really matters more to me?
- How can I live my life to reflect that?
- What are the possible consequences of not spending enough time on my real priorities?
- Am I prepared to risk those consequences? Why / why not?

Week 4 – Reflections of ourselves

Quick recap from the first three weeks:

We've done a lot of work already, and we should be getting a much better idea of what's really getting in the way of us being genuinely happy. Before we get started on this week's topic, let's do a quick recap of the 'Happy Workshop Principles' that we've learned so far:

Happy Workshop Principle 1:

Don't make your happiness depend on an external change in your circumstances. What if it never changes?
Instead, be happy with whatever your circumstances are, and look for all the good you already have in your life, however small.

Happy Workshop Principle 2:

Real happy doesn't come from externals. Real happy stays with you, even when things aren't going your way.

Happy Workshop Principle 3:

Live in the moment. Don't worry about tomorrow until you are there.

Happy Workshop Principle 4:

We can't control everything that happens to us, and neither can anyone else.

Happy Workshop Principle 5:

One of the key reasons we feel sad and depressed is because we have expectations that aren't being met.

Happy Workshop Principle 6:

The fewer expectations we have, the happier we will be.

Happy Workshop Principle 7:

We will only find genuine happiness once we figure out why we're REALLY unhappy.

With those seven Principles under our belt, we're ready to look at a subject that a lot of us find very difficult: our own faults and 'issues'.

Who are we really judging?

It's very hard for us to see ourselves objectively. We can always rationalize or explain away our own bad behaviour and bad characteristics, which can make it very hard for us to see how we are really acting, or what we really need to work on, to try and fix.

Luckily for us, 'Fate' has given us an amazing present: we are surrounded by people with every type of problem, 'issue' and negative characteristic trait, to show us what our own problems are.

It's a basic rule of thumb that you only notice the things in other people that you yourself have a problem with.

This might sound like a shocking idea – what?? I don't drive my car a million miles an hour like that homicidal lunatic in front of me! I always stand up to give the grannie my seat on the bus! I wouldn't dream of spending half my day on the phone to my girlfriend, like the guy in the next cubicle at work does!

While it's true that we may not be doing *exactly* the same actions as the homicidal speeding lunatic, or the selfish commuter, or the lazy work colleague, if their actions are bothering us, it's because on some level, we know we have a version of the same problem that we have to work on.

And this is not a new idea: remember the old adage, 'How you treat others is how you yourself will be treated'.

It's not just a nice thing to say – it's true.

Here's another old adage that makes the same point: 'Birds of a feather flock together'.

If you notice a bunch of negative character traits in the people you hang out with, or who you are related to, odds are you also have quite a few of the same ones yourself.

And the opposite is also true: if you notice a lot of amazingly positive things about your community, friends and family, then you probably also have quite a few of the same positive character traits yourself.

Making friends

I saw this for myself first hand, when I was talking to someone who has been finding it very difficult to make friends and integrate into the new community they moved to.

The person kept complaining that no-one was inviting them for a meal, or making an effort to make friends, so I asked her: "How many people have you invited over?" She looked at me blankly, so I repeated the question: how much effort had she been making to get acquainted with her neighbours?

The answer, it turned out, was 'very little'. But then, my friend went into defensive mode and tried to explain why it was still all the other people's 'fault'. "I'm new to the community," she said. "Everyone knows that when you move some place new, your neighbours are meant to come over and say hello, and bring you a cake or something."

She was right. That is the normal way of things. But I explained to her, she could either be 'right' or she could be 'happy' – but she couldn't be both.

This is such a fundamental concept when dealing with other people, that it's going to be our Happy Workshop Principle number 8:

Happy Workshop Principle 8:

When you're dealing with other people you can either choose to be 'right' – and to stand on principle – or you can choose to be 'happy'. But you normally can't choose both.

If you take a few minutes to think about it, and to be really honest with yourself, you can see for yourself that it's true.

We all know people that had a big fight with someone close to them, usually about something small and insignificant, and who are now trapped either in a cold war, where nobody talks to each other, or open hostilities.

Both parties will tell you until they are blue in the face about the other person's faults and problems; both parties are convinced of how 'right' they are, and will refuse to back down, or compromise or make up 'because of the principle of the thing'.

Sometimes, the best thing to do is to avoid the other person as much as possible, especially if we've been terribly and repeatedly hurt by them. But if it was a small thing? If it was a one-off? Then, the best route is nearly always to overlook the issue and make your peace.

When we have a good relationship with our family, friends, work colleagues and neighbours, we feel much more relaxed, much more loved, and much more happy.

All of this can be sacrificed when we stubbornly insist on being 'right'…

With that in mind, let's move on to our first exercise this week, where we're going to try to pinpoint what bugs us about other people.

Exercise 12 – What bugs us about other people

Take a few minutes, and on a clean sheet of paper, write down the main behaviours or characteristics of other people that really annoy you, or bug you, generally.

It might be helpful to split the list into two columns, one for 'family members' and one for everyone else.

[This next part only applies to parents:]

When you are done, turn the paper over, and make another list of your kids' character traits that really annoy you.

Example:

Do you find people to be:

- Bossy?
- Inconsiderate?
- Rude?
- Self-righteous?
- Complaining?
- Critical?
- Selfish?

What's my problem?

As we said at the beginning, it's very hard for us to 'see' ourselves and our behaviour objectively, because we always have a million good reasons and justifications for why we act the way we do.

But if you really want to know what your issues are, go back to the lists you made, particularly the list you made for your kids and / or family members and read them through carefully.

Exercise 13 – Things I need to work on

Take your lists, and star any of the characteristics that you recognize are really 'yours'. On a clean sheet of paper, write down the character traits that you starred, and call this new list 'Thing I need to work on'.

Over the next week, try and notice when you are displaying one or more of the character traits on this new list.

Don't expect to change or improve them overnight! The first part of the process is just to recognize that at least occasionally, you can also be bossy, or rude, or selfish – and that when you are, it has a negative impact on how happy you feel, and how nicely people treat you.

In a few weeks' time, we'll discuss what you can do to try and improve your negative character traits, but remember, real, lasting changes take time and cannot be rushed.

For now, we just want to build awareness of the Happy Workshop Principle number 9:

The issues that really get under our skin with other people is the stuff that we ourselves need to work on.

The other side of the coin

A few years' ago, I was making such a mess of looking after my then two year old, that I signed up for a whole bunch of parenting courses with a woman who'd raised eight kids, and married a lot of them off already.

She didn't mince her words, and called a spade a spade – which is why half the group kind of disappeared by class number 4.

But I loved her. I could see that she had a lot of wisdom, and I could also see that the things she was telling us were true, even if they were frequently quite uncomfortable truths.

One of the things she taught us was the principle of the 'other side of the coin'.

In short, she talked about how many, many people grow up in homes that are overly strict, or overly thrifty, or overly 'healthy – and then decide to go completely the other way when they grow up and have their own families.

These people tell themselves that they are 'never going to be how my parents were' – so they go to the other extreme, just to make sure. But when we go to the other extreme, all we are doing is setting up the pendulum to swing back to what we ourselves grew up with.

We all know people who grew up in very strict households who let their own kids run riot. Those kids grow up in turn, and revert back to strict rules and 'order', as a reaction to their own extremely chaotic childhoods.

Or, we all know people whose parents were macrobiotic health fanatics who now can't so much even look at a bowl of brown rice, and eat chocolate as a meal in and of itself. Fast forward 25 years, and their children are back steaming their broccoli and drinking mineral water.

Whenever behaviour is at an extreme, or is occurring as a reaction to what a person experienced in their own childhood, it's *essentially the same problem*. It's the same 'coin' – it's just the other side of it.

As you look through your lists, particularly your family lists, keep your eyes peeled for any of these 'other side of the coin' issues, as well as the more obvious ones.

Kids are our mirrors

The people in our lives who most reflect our own behaviour are our kids. It's a cast-iron rule that a couch potato kid will have a couch potato parent. A kid with a mean streak has a parent with a mean streak. A sweet kid with a good heart will have a sweet parent with a good heart.

Talk about pressure!

But the good news is that once you realize that *their* problem is really *your* problem, it's much easier and quicker to fix it. You don't need shrinks, medications, educational psychologists or expensive vacations.

All you need to do is to make a commitment to work on that particular character trait in yourself.

Exercise 14 – Your kid, your problem

[If you don't have kids, you can skip this exercise]

If you have kids, go back to your list of their character traits that annoy or upset you. Star the ones that are obviously 'you'. Put an exclamation mark next to the character traits that are obviously your spouse's (some of the same negative character traits may be present in both of you).

Now, think about how these traits are coming out in you and your spouse.

Example

Your child gets very despondent and / or upset and angry when they can't tie their shoelace properly; or if they don't understand their school work quickly; or if they can't get the puzzle pieces to fit the first time round.

This is usually a clear heads-up that one or both of the parents have 'perfectionist' tendencies. Even if you don't expect the child to do things 'perfectly' they will still expect it of themselves. Why? Because they are mirroring you!

If you want to really fix the problem at its root, you have to learn how to be more forgiving of your own errors and mistakes, and less stressed about those situations and occasions when things aren't going 100% to plan.

Seeing this in action

A little while ago, I started reading an excellent parenting book by top spiritual guide Shalom Arush, that really made me realize just how much work I still had to do to be a good parent.

As I read through the book, I collected more and more things that I needed to apologize to my kids about: I was sorry I still screamed at them; I was sorry that I was so quick to yell, and that I would frequently 'lose it' when it really wasn't a big deal.

One of my daughters – the one who is temperamentally the most similar to my husband – accepted my apology immediately. But my oldest daughter, who is almost a carbon copy of me, said that she had to think about whether she wanted to forgive me or not.

I was speechless! Before I really tried to internalize that my kids are just my mirror, I would have wasted hours trying to argue with my daughter about how unforgiving she was being, or trying to persuade her that forgiving me was the right thing to do, or trying to convince her that really, she didn't have a choice.

But instead of doing all that, I realized that I was being given a golden opportunity to have a good look at myself, and to 'catch' another negative character trait that I didn't realize I had.

I always thought that I was a fairly forgiving person, so it really took me by surprise that my daughter was not following suit. But I went and talked to my 'Higher Power' about it all, and within an hour I'd worked out that there are still a couple of people in my life that I was holding a grudge against.

I resolved to work on my problem, and to try to genuinely forgive them, then I went back to my house. Before I even asked her, my daughter came up to me and told me that she'd been thinking about my apology, and now she was happy to forgive me for screaming at her too much.

It was a real Eureka! moment. Once I noticed the problem in me and started trying to 'fix' it, it was automatically 'fixed' in my daughter, as well.

Exercise 15 – Fixing the problem

(If you have more than one list, ie, for family / kids / friends make sure that you write down all your starred character traits from across your different lists on one main master list, for this exercise.)

Look at your starred list of character traits you need to work on.

Pick the one character trait you'd like to work on over the course of the Happy Workshop (it might be an idea to make it a more 'minor' character trait, so you can practise these techniques and get the hang of it, before going for the really 'big' stuff).

Over the course of the next week, try to jot down every time you notice someone around you displaying that particular negative character trait.

Try to capture as much detail as you can: what was the situation? What happened? How did the person act or react? How did it appear to you, as the outsider? What would you have told them to do differently? Why? How do you think the people involved felt?

At the end of the week, go back over your notes, and try to internalize that when you yell at your kids, for example, it looks absolutely terrible to an outsider. They can see just how terrifying you look, just how scared your kids are, and just how much you've lost control.

Do you want to carry on being the person who loses it in the mini-market? Or the person who yells at the secretary when they get 'stressed' Or the person who starts having a massive argument on the side of the road with another driver?

When you get angry, you don't look any different from the angry people you've been watching all week.

Nobody respects a person like that. People try to avoid a person like that.

Do you want to carry on being that person?

Week 5 – Remembering that everyone is different

Today's modern world is so driven by mass-marketing and advertising that a lot of us – even most of us – have grown up with adverts and TV programs telling us who to be and how to think.

Close your eyes for a moment, and imagine a 'successful person'.

- How did that person look?
- What clothes was that person wearing?
- What car were they driving?
- What were they drinking?
- Where did they buy their groceries?
- Where did they live?

I can almost guarantee you that your successful person was not fat, or even a little bit chubby. I can also guarantee that they had great hair, white teeth, designer clothes and a fabulous beach house in Hawaii.

How do I know all this? Because I grew up watching the same movies and imbibing the same non-stop advertising that you did.

The adverts and the movies make us all want to look a certain way; they make us all want to aspire to live a certain lifestyle; to eat a particular brand of cornflakes; to drive a 'cool' car.

But what if that's just not 'you'?

What if you haven't got the money, or the figure, or the looks, or the kids, or the house, or the career, or the aspirations that you're supposed to have?

Then, you can get *really* miserable.

But only if you buy into the idea that we are all the same.

As soon as we try to understand that we are all individuals, and that we have all been created with different qualities, different abilities, different paths and missions in life, the picture looks amazingly different.

If you aren't blonde and thin, that's because your mission in life doesn't need you to be. If you can't carry a tune and have a tin ear, chances are you weren't created to be a pop star (although these days, that doesn't seem to stop a lot of people from trying…)

If you are rubbish at maths, bored by the small print and faint at the sight of blood, you clearly weren't meant to be a doctor, lawyer or accountant. There is a whole other amazing life journey mapped out for you.

The first step on that journey is to try to cut through all the mass media fuzz, all the expectations of the society we live in, and the families we were raised in, and to work out who we *really* are, and what we were *really* created to do, and to be.

So many people are so miserable today because their heads are full of ideas that aren't theirs, and 'ideals' that don't suit them or fit them at all.

In this chapter, we're going to try to get past the Hollywood-driven fantasy world to see who you really are. And what *you* really want to be when you grow up.

Putting down the mixing bowl

I've always been an 'individual'. Even when I was little, and desperate to fit in, I just never could. I always looked the wrong way, or dressed the wrong way, or lived in the wrong place, or spoke with the wrong accent. By the time I hit my late twenties, I thought I was happy being an oddball, and very comfortable with 'being different'.

I was sure that all my aspirations were 'mine', and that the life I wanted to lead was a logical choice, not a subconscious response to advertising, glossy magazines and movies.

Boy, was I wrong.

When I was 28, the pressures of having two small kids, very demanding clients and my own business was really starting to get to me. Although externally I was holding it together, inside I had this mounting feeling that I was approaching meltdown.

If something didn't change, soon, I felt very strongly I was going to crack up and lose everything I was working so hard to achieve. (In the end, I wasn't wrong, but we'll come on to that later...)

As part of my attempts to 'fix' this underlying worry and mounting stress, one of the many things I tried was Neuro Linguistic Programming (NLP). I had a few sessions with a nice man called Rob, who kept trying to get me to visualise things in a positive way, and to 're-program' my negative thought patterns.

In one of the visualisation exercises, Rob asked me to think about what my 'perfect life' looked like. It took a while to grab hold of the image that was kind of floating about in the back of my head, but when I did, I had a massive shock: the 'perfect me' was wearing a twin set, dressed in an apron, and holding a massive mixing bowl. It was pure 'perfect 50s mom' – and it didn't reflect the real me at all.

The real me wore jeans and sweat shirts all the time. The real me wasn't in to baking cookies as a hobby. The real me had crazy, wild hair – the exact opposite of the perfectly-groomed woman in my mental picture.

No wonder I was feeling like a miserable failure so much of the time! My internal 'picture' of who I should try to be was completely different from who I really was.

The Neuro Linguistic Programming helped to put a temporary sticking plaster over my problems, but apart from giving me that key insight in to what was really underneath a lot of my issues, long-term, it was a waste of time.

Because the real problem was that I was trying to be something I wasn't, and something I could never be.

The next hard question I had to ask myself was: where the heck had this ridiculous idea of how I 'should be' come from?

It took me months and years to work it out, but the light-bulb went on when I saw a re-run of a Grace Kelly movie call High Society, that I'd watched over and over again as a kid. The blonde, elegant, waspy Grace Kelly was the 'perfect' me, right down to her twinset, pearls and hairdo!

But I'm a Jew. I have black hair. I don't live in a mansion with a swimming pool and hang out with singing celebrities…

Once I realized that the 'ideal' I'd been trying to subconsciously emulate was a Hollywood fantasy that I'd seen when I was six years old, it was such a relief. It helped me to let go of so many negative mental comparisons that had just been dragging me down, and making me feel miserable. I didn't have to wear a twin set and pearl earrings and be a size 10 and have perfectly set, straight blonde hair to be happy anymore.

I was constantly failing at all these things because they were never 'me' to begin with. The real 'me' loves being a bit scruffy, and will put comfort over appearance every single time. The real 'me' has a big bottom – and always will, no matter what I eat or how much I exercise.

The real 'me' can't stand beach holidays, cruises or five-star buffets. The real 'me' thinks that long fingernails are completely pointless – how the heck can you write, or take your contact lenses out, or tie your shoelaces?

The real 'me' always believed that there was more to life than making and spending money, and 'looking good' - but somewhere along the way, I forgot who the real 'me' was.

Once I let go of that 'fake' ideal, I could start to work on creating something real to aim at, something that was based on who I really was, and what I really wanted to try to do with my life.

And I was so much happier as a result.

We're going to try to do the same for you now, with our next set of exercises.

Exercise 16 – The Media Diary

Take a clean sheet of paper, and divide it into a seven day grid. Put the seven days of the week down one side of the grid, and then divide the rest of the table into two sections. Mark one section: 'Media' and mark the second section: 'How I felt afterwards'.

Over the coming week, every time you read a newspaper or magazine, listen to the radio, watch TV or a movie, play a computer game, or surf the net, write down what you watched, read, played, or listened to, and then think about how you felt afterwards.

At the end of the week, look back over your media diary, and see what media experiences were genuinely positive, and which experiences were not.

A positive media experience leaves gives you inspiration, or strength, or food for thought long after it's finished.

A negative media experience leaves you shaken, scared, worried, anxious, self-loathing, dissatisfied or 'disconnected' from the real world. You have a yucky feeling afterwards, that can take hours, days or even weeks and months to get rid of, depending on how 'strong' your reaction was.

Once you start to notice how the media is really affecting your mood, state of mind, and how you relate to your own life, ask yourself:

- Are there any changes I want to make to my media habits?
- If I recognize that certain things are making me feel miserable, how can I best minimise them, or cut them out of my life altogether?
- What, if anything, is making me feel good, or positive about myself? Why?
- What's stopping me from changing my bad media habits?

Example

On Sunday, Janice read through the weekend paper. After the news section, she felt quite apprehensive, particularly about the state of the economy and the spiralling street crime figures.

Next, she read the travel section, which inspired her to look into checking out cheaper, more unusual options for her next holiday – holidays didn't have to mean hotels with swimming pools!

Next, she read the women's magazine insert, and came away feeling dissatisfied on a few counts: she really liked the 'handbag of the month' they were showcasing – but it was completely out of her price range.

She read the 'bathroom makeover' – and that made her want to get new towels and bathroom accessories for her own place, but again, she couldn't really afford the luxury brands being advertised in the makeover, and was already fretting about where she could find cheaper versions that would be 'good enough'.

The feature on the 'must have mini-skirt' also made her feel down, as Janice feels she'd have to lose a lot of weight before she could look good in a mini.

In her media diary, she writes:

Sunday: Weekend Paper
        News section   Anxious; worried; scared
        Travel section   Inspired; excited
        Womens' Pullout Depressed; dissatisfied; lacking

Example

Greg got his Facebook account a couple of years' ago to keep up with family news. He doesn't live close to his parents and siblings, and he thought it would be a great way of staying in touch easily.

Greg spends at least an hour on Facebook every night – and more often than not, he comes away from his internet session feeling quite down and introspective.

Recently, he's got back in touch with a lot of old school friends, and they seem to be having a much better life than him.

They are continually posting up pictures from their latest holidays, or describing their new, amazing jobs, or sharing how 'fabulous' their latest romantic night out was, or boasting about how well their kids are doing in school.

Greg doesn't like his job but hasn't been able to find anything else because of the recession. Greg is going through a rough patch with his wife, exacerbated by his work issues, and his sense of loneliness, from being so far away from his family. Greg feels that he needs a lot more support than he's getting.

Reading about everyone else's 'perfect lives' makes him feel even more dissatisfied with his own problems.

But he feels a bit more in touch with his parents and wider family, and he loves reading his siblings' posts, and seeing the photos of his nieces and nephews.

In his media diary, he writes:

Tues: **Facebook**

- Happy to catch up with family
- Miserable I don't live closer
- Jealous that people seem to be making more   money / have better jobs
- A bit sorry for myself, that I'm not going on a five star cruise to Sweden
- Trying to think what I can post up about my life... - maybe something about my garden?

****

We don't have to continue to read, watch or listen to things that make us miserable, just because 'everyone else' is doing it.

If a particular media really isn't working for you, don't be afraid to cut it out for a day, a week, or a month, to see just how much it's affecting your mood and outlook.

It sounds like a radical idea, but if listening to the news brings you down and makes you worry, stop listening to it! You'll still find out everything you really need to know about, and you'll quickly realize that 99% of what's called 'news' is actually just opinion, conjecture and scare mongering.

Who needs it?

Happy Workshop Principle 10:

If movies, Facebook and newspapers are making you miserable, then take a break and either reduce them significantly, or cut them out altogether.

Free press, or 'de'-pressed

This book is not the place to go into a detailed discussion of what is so wrong with today's media and why it makes so many people so unhappy. But we do need to understand a bit more about how it's affecting our thought processes, and by extension, our mood, so that we can make a conscious, informed decision about how much media we really want to have in our lives.

Most of today's media works on the Superior / Inferior principle.

When we read articles about poor, flood-hit countries, scumbag parents and drug-addict celebrities, we get a kick out of the fact that *we are better than that.*

But then, when we read articles about France's amazing socialised healthcare, or the latest business exec who is being paid $10 million, or the 'Powerhouse mum' who has six kids and has also just singlehandedly turned around an inner city school – we get down, because *we aren't that good.*

This is the Superior / Inferior principle. The next time you flip through a newspaper, or visit a friend's Facebook page, pay attention and see just how much of what you are taking in is hinged around these two ideas.

OK, so now we hit a big question: what's so bad about it?

Why is it such a big deal, and how does the Superior / Inferior principle really affect me, and my attempts to be happy?

Great question! Grab a clean sheet of paper, and the next exercise will help us to answer it.

Exercise 17: Superior / Inferior complex

Take a few minutes, and write down how you feel **when you are successful.**

You got promoted; you scored the winning goal; your kid is top of the class; you just got a nice new kitchen; you won the lottery; you lost 30 lbs – how do you feel?

[NB, try not to look at the Happy Workshop answers until you've done your own list, as otherwise you may not get an accurate picture of what is really going on inside your own head...]

When we are winning, when we are successful, we feel:

- Smug
- Proud
- Superior - we look down at other people who haven't achieved what we have

- Judgemental – we make a lot of judgement calls about all the 'losers' who aren't making enough effort; or who aren't trying hard enough; or who are lazy, inconsiderate, or 'irresponsible' –(a great key word for people who think they run the world)
- Arrogant – 'My kids would never act like that!' I would never leave the house like that! I would never let that happen! I would never screw up such an important business meeting! etc etc.

The trouble is, nobody is infallible. All of us, even the most conscientious, gifted, talented person around can and does make mistakes.

If we're really honest, we'll admit that when things go our way, it's because 'Fate' is helping us out. There are plenty of people who work just as hard, who try just as hard, who are even more clever and even more conscientious than we are – and it still just doesn't work out for them.

Now, turn your sheet of paper over, and write down how you feel when you are failing. What happens when:

- You didn't get the job;
- Your proposal was rejected;
- Your girlfriend broke up with you;
- Your kid is failing badly in school;
- You can't keep up with the mortgage payments;
- You can't afford even a weekend away.

How do you feel?

[Write down your own ideas before you continue.]

Even if we try to cover it up and pretend 'we don't care', or 'it's just one of those things', or 'it was so-and-so's fault' – what we are really feeling is:

- Worthless
- Defensive
- Edgy
- Miserable
- Depressed
- Despairing – it's never going to change; nothing I do ever goes right etc
- Angry – why couldn't it be different?
- Bitter – out to blame everything and everyone for our own problems and failings

For now, we aren't going to talk about what we can actually do about all these negative feelings. It's enough just to start recognizing them, and to start realizing what particular media is pressing what particular button.

If I'm honest, there are times when I still find it hard to stay away from all the glossy cooking or home furnishings magazines. The pictures are sooooo pretty. The food is soooo imaginative. The houses are sooooo gorgeous – but as the years go on, it's getting easier and easier to skip the magazine isle.

I know all the movies and mags and You tube clips are attractive to look at. I know I could enjoy them immensely for a whole five minutes. And I also know that as soon as I put the magazine down, or turn the computer off, I'm going to be spending the next 10 months comparing my 'imperfectly real' life to the media's 'perfectly fake' version – and feeling bad about myself.

These days, I'm simply not prepared to let all the media's 'perfectly fake' make me feel miserable about my imperfect, but actually really great real life.

Week 6 – Seeing the good

The last few weeks, we've been digging out a lot of the rubbish in our sub-conscious that has been making us miserable, and dragging us down. It's been hard work, but remember the Happy Workshop Principle Number 7:

Happy Workshop Principle 7:

We will only find genuine happiness once we figure out why we're REALLY unhappy.

If you've been doing the exercises as we go along, you probably already have a much better idea of some of the things that are getting in the way of you being genuinely happy.

This week, we're going to take a step back, and we're going to try to approach 'happy' from the other side.

We're going to go back to our Happy Workshop Principle Number 2, and explore it in more detail:

Happy Workshop Principle 2:

Real happy doesn't come from externals. Real happy stays with you, even when things aren't going your way.

How can we be happy, really happy, if:

- We still haven't met the man or woman of our dreams?
- We're still out of work?
- We're still struggling with serious health problems?
- Our life looks terribly bleak and black?

The answer is very simple: we have to look at all the good that we *do* have in our lives.

Taking life for granted

A couple of years' ago, I heard a story where a father was trying to raise two million dollars to pay for his son to have a highly-complicated, specialised surgery done on his hands.

The son had been born with the fingers on both hands fused together, which meant that he effectively had 'flippers', and couldn't use his hands in any practical, effective way.

There was a surgeon in Germany who could perform the surgery, and the man was going around Israel trying to raise the money for the operation. In the process, he went to visit a well-known Rabbi, to get a blessing for the forthcoming operation.

After the visit, the Rabbi publicised the story to help the man raise funds – but also, to encourage people to recognize their own blessings.

Each working, ordinary hand was worth a million dollars to this man and his son.

Just think: if you can move your fingers; if you can type; or hold a toothbrush; or dial a phone number - your own two hands are worth $2 million!

But who's grateful that their hands work?

Do you remember the little Iraqi boy who lost both his arms when the US Airforce accidentally bombed his home, when President Bush Jnr was trying to track down Saddam Hussein?

The first time I saw pictures of that little, arm-less boy, I cried buckets and buckets. How was he going to get dressed in the mornings? How was he going to climb trees or play ball with his friends? How was he going to work? How was he going to live? What could he do with his life, without his arms?

Thankfully, a lot of money was raised, and the last I heard, he was taken to America, outfitted with the latest limb technology and has a lot of plans and ambitions for the future.

But when was the last time you said thank you that you have both of your arms?

When is the last time you were grateful that your heart works fine, or that you don't need to be hooked up to a kidney dialysis machine three times a week, or that you can actually taste your food?

When is the last time you were grateful that you had a roof over your head, or a comfy chair to sit in, or food in the fridge?

Remember those South American miners, who were trapped underground for weeks and weeks, while the rescue teams were working day and night to free them? Just imagine how it felt, stuck in the same dark, stinking hole for day after day after day.

No-one could go for a walk. No-one could get a 'change of scene'. No-one could watch the sunrise, or see the sunset. No one could sit in the park and watch the flowers in bloom.

Every breath of air is a free gift, a present.

But so many of us overlook the tremendous blessings that we already have, in the mad chase for 'more' and 'different' and 'better'. Our heads are full of all the clothes we want to buy, and all the holidays we want to book, and all the 'experiences' we want to have.

There's a Jewish saying that a person dies with not even half of their wants fulfilled.

What this means, practically, is that if we spend our whole life making our happiness dependent on getting the things that we want – we'll never be happy.

Why?

Because our list of 'wants' is never-ending. As soon as we buy a new car, or a new house, or a new outfit, the novelty value has already worn off by the next day, and a new 'want' has moved up to the top of the list.

One of the single biggest secrets of genuine happiness is to recognize what we already have, and to be grateful for it.

It's such a key thing, that we are going to make it our Happy Workshop Principle Number 11:

Happy Workshop Principle 11:

Real happiness begins when you start to appreciate all the good you already have in your life.

It works for 'big' stuff, too...

A lot of people might read Principle 11, and think to themselves that maybe all this stuff works when people already have a nice life, but it just can't work when you're struggling with massive problems.

If a person is terminally sick, or going through a divorce, or going bankrupt, or has a drug-addict kid – they don't have anything to be really happy about. Who cares that their hands work, or that they can see, or that they just went for a nice walk in a forest?!?!?

A lot of people who are struggling with massive problems think this way – but it's wrong.

It's precisely when things get tough that you **must** look for all the good that you still have in your life.

If you don't, what's the alternative?

Depression. Despair. Blackness. Drugs. Misery. And when people can't see any way out, and can't stand their suffering any more, suicide.

All of us have struggles in life. All of us, even rich people; even 'successful' people; even thin, beautiful people. When those difficulties strike, they can capsize us, unless we cling on to all of the good that we still have in our life.

OK, I'm not jumping up and down that I lost my job, but thank God, I'm still healthy!

It's not great that I have chronic back pain all the time, but at least I have a loving family who are doing their best to take care of me…
My kids just spilt Ribena on the new carpet and it's stained. But I'm so grateful I have healthy kids in the first place! I know of so many people who are struggling to get pregnant, or who never found 'Mr Right' in time to start a family….

Each of can choose to be happy. All we have to do is to stop focussing on the thing or things that are going 'wrong', and to look at all the hundreds of things in our lives that are still going right.

Remember Happy Workshop Principle Number 2:

Happy Workshop Principle 2:

Real happy doesn't come from externals. Real happy stays with you, even when things aren't going your way.

But most of us aren't used to thinking that way.

We need a bit of help to start focussing on the good, which brings us very nicely to this week's exercises.

Exercise 18 – The good things notebook

For this exercise, you'll need some sort of notebook or writing pad – loose sheets of paper won't really do, unless you stick them in a binder and are really disciplined about keeping them all together in the same place.

You should only try and do this exercise when you are in more upbeat or positive frame of mind. If you're already down or depressed, wait a day or two until you feel a bit happier about life.

Once you've got started on your 'good things' notebook, you can take it out and go over it if you feel an attack of the 'blahs' about to hit you – you'll be amazed how quickly your mood lifts, and how fast you start to feel more optimistic about life again.

The premise of the 'good things' notebook is very simple: over the course of the next week, write down everything that's good in your life. They can be 'big' goods, like the fact that you just bought a new car; or aced a crucial exam, or got over a nasty illness; but the vast majority of the notebook should consist of the 'small' goods that all of us have in abundance, but don't always notice.

If someone holds a door open for you, write it down. If your kid smiles a sweet smile, or says something cute, write it down. If a friend calls you, or your mum sends you an email, write it down.

More ideas for your 'good things' notebook

- Your shower works, and you have enough hot water for a nice, long wash
- You can have a cup of coffee – in your favourite mug – whenever the mood takes you
- The bulbs you planted in your garden are starting to bloom
- You had an umbrella in your bag, so you didn't get soaked in the unexpected downpour
- You woke up today (not everyone does...)
- You woke up today next to someone you love
- Someone you love woke you up in the middle of the night because they had a bad dream
- You're wearing a really comfortable pair of shoes (have you ever tried to walk around in shoes that rub and give you blisters? Torture...)
- Apart from the odd cold or bout of flu, you haven't had any serious health issues for years
- It rained today (and your country is in the middle of a drought...)
- It didn't rain today – and everything looked so beautiful in the sunlight
- You got a seat on the bus
- You didn't get a seat on the bus – but you're healthy and young, so it wasn't hard to stand up for the whole journey
- Someone taught you how to read (millions of people in the world are illiterate...)
- You fought with your sister (at least you have one...)
- You made up with your sister
- Your husband came home early from work to spend some time with you
- Your husband came home late from work (at least he's making a living...)

- You can breathe just fine
- You can swallow (remember how hard it is when you have sore throat?)
- You're making your favourite supper tonight
- You went for a walk

You get the idea.

The more you train yourself to see all the good that's all around you, the more good you'll notice. You'll notice when one of your colleagues does something nice for you at work; or when your have a warm sweater to wear on a cold day; or your car works every time you turn it on.

Things could be so different.

There is no time limit for the 'good things' notebook. Do it for at least a week, but you can keep it going for as long as you want. Every day, you'll find new things to appreciate and be grateful for.

Instead of living a miserable life of 'lack' and disappointment, you'll have a whole book – maybe even a library of books – of things to be happy about.

If you're having a bad day, go back and read through your 'good things' notebook, and make an effort to see the good in your life. Don't get stuck just obsessing about 'the problem' or issue. Your life is so much bigger than that.

Good points

No-one is perfect. If a person never said 'sorry' in their life, that doesn't mean that they are a 'perfect', or perfectly good person – it just means that they never accepted the fact that they also make mistakes.

But by the same token, no-one is completely 'bad', either. All of us, even the worst person in the world, has some good in them.

It's a known fact that people who can see the good in others, and who can see the good in *themselves,* are much happier people.

Why?

Firstly, because instead of seeing the world as a bleak place, populated by horrible people who are out to get them, the people who focus on the 'good points' really know just how much good is actually out there.

The world is full of people delivering meals on wheels; or coaching a soccer game in their free time; or phoning a friend to make them feel good; or making their spouses a millionth cup of tea.

The second reason is that once you start to find all the good that's hidden in you, you realize – all of a sudden – just how much you really can, and really do, affect the world for the good.

Every time you pick up a piece of rubbish from the pavement, you are building the world. Every time you smile at the check-out girl, you are building the world. Every time you give up your seat on a busy bus or train to someone who needs it more than you do – you are building the world.

And all those small, but beautiful, good points are the foundation that the world is built on. Without you, and your small kindnesses, things would fall apart very fast.

And if that doesn't make a person feel genuinely happy, and feel that their life – and the life of those around them - has genuine worth and value, then I don't know what does.

Happy Workshop Principle 11:

The more kindnesses we do for others, the more kindness and goodness we'll recognize in the world, and the happier we'll feel.

So let's see just how many amazing good points you have, in the next exercise.

Exercise 19 – Finding our good points

Take a clean piece of paper, and write 'my good points' in a circle in the middle. The easiest way to 'catch' your good points is to split your life up in to categories. In my 'good points' mind map, I'm going to divide my life according to the different roles I play.

So I'll draw lines off the 'my good points' centre circle called:

- Mum
- Wife
- Daughter

- Sister
- In-law
- Friend
- Work Colleague
- Neighbour

Under each category, I'm going to list my relevant good points. Again, the point is to be as detailed as possible, and to write down even the small 'good things' that fill our day.

Under Mum, I write down:

- Make three meals a day
- Help with homework
- Make the time to talk to my kids when they come home from school
- Skimp on things that I want to buy, so that we can afford the things they need to have
- Tidy their rooms when they get too messy
- Tell them 'I love you' at least once a day – and mean it

You get the idea.

Go through each category, and list your good points. Are you a patient spouse? A generous boss? A great listener? Did you help your neighbour change a flat tyre?

Write it all down, and you'll start to see just what a world of 'good' you are building around you.

What happens if I can't find any good points?

Sometimes, we fall to such a low place, that we struggle to find any good in ourselves.

If that sounds like you, remember, you only need to find one 'good point' to turn the whole picture around, and start the journey back to being a happy, fulfilled person again.

Everyone has some good in them.

Everyone.

Including you.

Did you once do something nice for your mum? Did you ever buy your wife a bunch of flowers? Did you take your kid to the zoo? Did you knock yourself out at work to try and provide a living for your family? Did you hold your tongue when you really wanted to yell at someone? Did you try to cheer up a friend who was having a bad day? Or stop at a crossing to let a pedestrian have the right of way?

Don't stop looking until you find that one good thing that is inside you.

And then, start to build on it.

You may have done a lot of bad things up until now. Most of us have. The way to start to fix it all is by doing more good.

There is a spiritual rule that if we believe *we* broke something, we have to believe that *we* have the power to fix it. A little later on, we'll discuss the subject of how to fix things that we broke – even the big, enormous things we never want to talk about or own up to- in more detail.

But for now, focus on doing as many acts of kindnesses as you can. Each additional act of kindness will make you feel a whole lot happier, better, and more at peace with yourself, and the world around you.

Week 7 – Stop beating yourself up

We're at week seven in the Happy Workshop. If you've been doing the exercises, you'll already have a good idea about:

- What's really making you miserable
- What really makes you happy
- Which 'outside' influences are affecting your state of mind
- How your attitudes about other people are really affecting your own happiness
- What your good points are, and
- How many big and small kindnesses you have in your life every single day

This week, we're going to look at another prime cause of sadness and depression: Beating Ourselves Up disease.

But first, a story...

A little while ago, I was having a really hard few weeks. A lot of the things I'd been trying to do had stalled, or were failing, and I was starting to forget a lot of the 'Happy Workshop' principles that keep me happy and positive.

Initially, I didn't take all my setbacks and failures so much to heart, but when things seemed to be 'stuck' in quite a negative phase – and I was failing in a lot of different areas of my life all at once – that feeling that I'd 'dropped the ball' somewhere, and must be doing things wrong, started to intensify.

After a couple of days of small, nagging doubts, boom – I found myself in the middle of a full-blown 'beating myself up' attack.

We all know how that feels. We make a mistake; or something 'bad' happens to us; or we hear some bad news; or we don't manage to accomplish something we were really keen to do – and all of a sudden, that voice in our head starts berating us:

"You're a failure! You're a loser! Things are *never* going to change or improve, you're just wasting your time. Things are bad! Things are terrible! Things are only going to get worse- and **it's all your fault...**"

Sometimes, we really do make mistakes, and we really do have to learn from them, and to decide to try and do things differently or better next time. But most of the time? Most of the time, we are already doing the best we can, there was nothing we could or would have done differently, and things don't work out for us simply because 'Fate' decided otherwise.

Can you see into the future? Do you know which job is going to work out best? What school is really the best fit for your kid? What chance remark is going to lead to the worst argument you've had in 20 years? What reaction you are going to get for every action you make?

I certainly can't.

We all like to think that we control our lives, and every small detail in them. But that's simply not true. Most of us can't even control if we'll get to work on time – there are so many 'outside' factors affecting it, from bad weather to accidents to over-heating engines, to terrible traffic – and that's just all the external stuff that's happening outside of our homes.

So many of us are told that we can 'make it happen' and that all it takes is hard work and dedication to the task. But if we're really honest with ourselves, and we take a long, hard look at some of the things that are not going our way, we'll see that the only thing we really have control over is how we react to the situations we find ourselves in.

Everything else is out of our hands.

Remember Happy Workshop Principle number 4:

Happy Workshop Principle 4:

We can't control everything that happens to us, and neither can anyone else.

The people who really internalize this don't waste their time beating themselves up.

Yes, they look back at the situation or circumstance and they see if there is anything they can learn, or improve or do differently the next time round.

For example, if I'm constantly yelling at my kids at bedtime because they are over-tired and cranky by the time they actually need to go to sleep, then I have to think about how I can change our routine to make the whole 'bedtime' experience more pleasant for everyone.

Can I bring bedtime forward? Be stricter about sending friends home after a certain time? Make sure I get supper ready earlier? Etc

If I'm constantly binging on potato chips on the way home from work, I need to think about what changes I could make in my eating habits so that I'm not starving hungry with nothing to eat but junk food.

Can I make an extra sandwich? Pack an apple? Eat a bigger lunch later in the day? Etc

I hurt someone's feelings because I was too honest with them. This happens a lot. I need to think about how I can express my views in a more sensitive way that won't hurt the people I'm talking to and care about.

Can I avoid these types of conversation, unless I know the person is really ready to hear what I think? Is what I think actually right? Is it useful to be telling them what I think, even if I am being 'honest'?

This type of introspection leads to positive changes, and is something that most of us don't do anywhere near enough of.

But it's **not** beating ourselves up.

In fact, it's the opposite of beating ourselves up – because when we beat ourselves up, and go on and on about how stupid we were, or how careless we were, or how mean we were – then, we think we took care of the '*mea culpa*' bit, and we give ourselves permission to carry on doing exactly the same 'mistake' again next time.

When we don't beat ourselves up, and instead devote a few minutes to really thinking the situation through, and really asking ourselves some tough questions about what, honestly, we can do about it all – that is the beginning of a solution.

It's also the beginning of more self-awareness that a lot of the things that are 'hard' for us, or 'bad' for us – and by extension, the people around us - are really only 'bad' because of how we react to them.

A person may have a bad day at work, but if they feel that the 'bad day' they had gives them permission to scream at their spouse and kids when they get home– they are fooling themselves.

When we start to think these difficult situations through, and to break them down into their component parts, all of a sudden we get a much clearer picture of what's really going on in our lives, and what changes we really need to make.

The 'Bad Day' breakdown

Let's walk through the 'bad day' scenario:

You had a lousy day at work, because your boss embarrassed you in front of your colleagues, and tried to blame you for a mistake they made.

Understandably, it was a very unpleasant, stressful situation, and you were boiling over, but felt you couldn't argue against your boss without potentially putting your job on the line – and in this tough economic climate, it's not going to be easy to get another job.

You came home, still furious, and just wanted to sit quietly with a coffee for a few minutes, and 'unwind'. Your teenager came in, dumped their stuff all over the floor (something that you've asked them not to do a hundred times) – and you exploded at them.

You yelled, you screamed, you cursed. All the bitterness, the anger, the upset from the day came out – at your teenager. The teenager turned tail and fled upstairs. Even though you calmed down an hour ago, and you've tried to say 'sorry' through their locked door, they aren't responding.

And in your secret soul, you know that it's going to take a lot more than a 'sorry' to repair the damage that's just been done.

Where do you go from here?

Response 1: Beat yourself up

Most of us, faced with this scenario, would feel terrible for at least a few hours afterwards. We'll tell ourselves we are terrible parents. We'll blame the horrible job and boss for putting us into such a stressful situation. We'll try to say 'sorry' a few times – and then get really upset with our children if they aren't willing to accept our apology first time around.

Don't they understand the pressure I'm under? Don't they know how hard it is to come back to a messy house after a hard day in the office? They don't appreciate me. They don't appreciate all the things I do for them. They are horrible, ungrateful people - just like my boss!!!

We start by beating ourselves up, and we finish by beating up everyone else around us.

The end result of all the beating ourselves up is:

- We still feel terrible about ourselves
- We feel very sad, down, depressed and / or despairing that the situation is ever going to change or improve
- We feel very isolated, particularly from the people we most love
- We have no solution to our problem, and our reaction has compounded the issues we are facing. Now, as well as a problem with our boss, we also have a problem with our **kid**
- Because we feel so horrible about ourselves we always feel edgy and on the defensive, particularly around those people that keep pressing up against our issues (usually our spouse and children)
- The more defensive we are, the more stressed we feel, the more invisible barriers we put up between us and the people we love, the more lonely, sad and despairing we get, the more arguments we have….

And so on and so forth.

So what would be a better way of approaching the exact same scenario?

Response 2: Do some honest introspection

Honest introspection is like trying to solve a murder mystery: you go back to the scene of the crime, and you gather the bits of evidence, and carefully examine the 'clues' until you build up an accurate picture of **what really happened, and why.**

STEP 1:

Be honest. Set down what happened and why – and be aware that you have a vested interest in exonerating yourself.

If you make it someone else's problem or issue when it's really your own problem or issue – you are going to keep finding yourself in the same, unpleasant, stressful and unhappy situations.

In our 'Bad Day' scenario, the cold, hard facts are as follows:

- The boss acted terribly towards you and embarrassed you in front of your colleagues
- He blamed you for a mistake that he himself made
- You didn't or couldn't defend yourself or answer back
- You came home very wound up
- You took it out on the first person that came into your orbit – your teenager
- Your teenager is really hurt and upset with you, because you completely over-reacted

So far, so good. Let's continuing our snooping, and start asking ourselves some questions.

STEP 2:

Try to objectively analyse what happened, and why:

Fact 1: The boss's bad behaviour

- Was it a one off, or does it happen a lot?
- Does it only happen to you, or to other people as well?
- Is the boss generally a nice person to work with, or not?
- Has their behaviour changed or deteriorated recently?
- Are you aware of anything in their work or private life that might be 'stressing them out'?

If the boss is always horrible and rude to you, you might be getting a clear message to start looking for a new job (which you might not want to hear…)

If it was a one-off, and the boss has otherwise been good to work for, they were probably also having a 'bad day'. That doesn't excuse the behaviour, but it's not an automatic cue to switch jobs.

Fact 2: They blamed you for a mistake they made

Again, does this happen a lot? Does it happen to other people? If it also happens to other people – it's the boss, and there's not much you can do about it.

The upside of this situation is that no-one else will take the boss's criticism and blame seriously – if it's happened to a lot of other people, you'll actually get a lot of 'office sympathy' for being the latest victim.

If it's a one-off, and they are generally approachable and open, go and talk to them about it. Maybe it was a genuine error, or oversight? Maybe they really thought you had done something wrong?

Maybe you really *did* do something wrong, and hadn't realized?

Fact 3: You couldn't answer back

Again, if you really want to get a clear picture of what is going on, you have to ask yourself some tough questions: why couldn't you answer back? What was stopping you? Do you ever answer back? Do you ever stand up for yourself?

Do you only have that problem at work, with that boss, or does it crop up in other situations as well?

How did you feel about not being able to answer back?

What could you do to change it, if it happens again in the future?

How much of your anger at home resulted from feeling you couldn't express yourself, or defend yourself at work?

What 'old issues' is this pressing up against?

Fact 4: You came home very wound up

Could you have gone somewhere else first, to unwind a bit before you got home? Could you have gone for a coffee with a friend? Could you have gone for a jog, or worked out in the gym, or gone for a long walk around the local park?

If you just wanted to sit at home and think, was downstairs the best place? Could you have found a more quiet, more private spot? Do you need to think about creating one, so have a 'haven' to come home to, where you can unwind?

Fact 5: You took it out on your teenager

Yes, it would be great if they would listen more and cooperate more and be more responsive.

But how did you used to act, when you were a teenager? Did you always do everything that your parents told you? Were there times when you didn't listen to them, not to be spiteful, but just because you forgot, or didn't think it was important, or even, because you disagreed with them?

Were you able to discuss things with your own parents, or were you always forced to do what they said?

How did you feel, when they made you do something, or yelled at you?

Is this something that keeps happening with your kids and spouse? Or with that kid in particular?

Why?

Fact 6: You over-reacted, and your teenager is very upset with you

Does this happen a lot? Is it a one-off?

Can you talk to your teenager, and explain that you realize you didn't act appropriately?

Kids are usually far more 'fair' and honest than their parents, and they already know you aren't perfect. If you own up to your mistakes, and explain that you want to change things but you don't always know how, you'll get a lot more respect from them. You may also get a solution that really works…

Put yourself in their shoes: if someone had just yelled at you, what would it take to smooth things over and make it good again?

If you can't or won't apologize, what's stopping you?

Do you really want to have a good relationship with your kids?

STEP 3:

The conclusion.

At the end of this process of honest introspection, you should have a lot more clarity about what is really going on, and what, really, you can do about it.

Your boss is generally a nice person, but they were very close to a family member who just died, and they took it very hard.

You don't need to look for a new job (unless it starts to happen on a regular basis...) but you do need to make an appointment to go and talk it through with them and 'air it out'.

You hate confrontations – which is why you didn't say anything in the meeting – but you now realize that if you don't address the problem with your boss, you are going to continue to feel stressed and uncomfortable at work, which will lead to much more stress in the home, as well.

When you're stressed, you yell at people. You need at least an hour to unwind from work after a 'bad day' and you decide to either go to the gym for a work-out, or to clear out the spare room and turn it into a study, where you can lock the door and have some private time to clear your head without anyone bothering you (or you attacking them).

You want a good relationship with your kids, but it's very hard for you to admit that you make mistakes and do things 'wrong' sometimes. You realize there is no 'quick fix' for this, and that you just have to keep working on yourself.

You also understand that the 'price' of not saying sorry and being honest with your teenager is an increasingly tense and distant relationship. You don't want that, because a kid who's unhappy at home will spend more and more time on the street – doing all sorts of things you don't even want to think about.

This is what gives you the 'push' to swallow your pride, and to make an effort to give your kid a proper, sincere apology and explanation for your behaviour.

Happy Workshop Principle 12:

Instead of pointlessly beating ourselves up about our mistakes and failures, we need to 'solve the mystery' and do some honest introspection to find out what's really going on, why, and what we can do about it.

Exercise 20: What am I beating myself up about?

On a clean sheet of people, write down some of the things that you've been beating yourself up about over the last week or two.

- Did you fall off your diet?
- Did you have an argument with your sister?
- Did you make a promise you didn't keep?
- Did you steal the credit for someone else's project at work?

Whatever it is, big or small, pick one, and work it through, following the three step 'honest introspection' process we've just outlined above.

STEP 1: State the facts as objectively as you can

Stay away from explanations or rationalisations at this point. Stick to what actually happened, and save the 'why' for Step 2:

STEP 2: Ask yourself some questions, including some 'hard' questions, to find out what really happened

Don't be scared to ask yourself if you're at fault, or doing something wrong. So many people are trapped in miserable lives or miserable circumstances because they refuse to admit their problems or failings.

We are all human beings. None of us are angels, or act perfectly 100% of the time. If you've never said sorry, or never 'caught' yourself doing something wrong or bad, it's not because you never did it – you just never owned up to it.

Even good people occasionally make some bad mistakes. Don't be scared to admit them, because then you can take whatever action is required to clean up the mess you made.

Things can always be fixed. But the longer you leave it, the bigger it gets, and the harder it will be to sort it all out.

People will love you much more for being an honest, imperfect person who's trying their best than if you try to be a 'perfect person' who never admits that they are wrong.

STEP 3: Draw a conclusion, and work out where you go from there

Do you need to change something? Is there a conversation you need to have? A circumstance that needs to be different, an improvement that needs to be made? What needs to disappear from – or be added into – your daily routine?

What have you realized about yourself that you never knew before?

Are you happy with the status quo, or do you really want something different? How can you achieve it?

What did you do wrong?

Who do you need to say sorry to, and why?

What happens if I've drawn my conclusion, but I know I just can't change or do what's required to 'fix' the situation?

First of all, you're not alone. All of us, at some point, will come up against a situation of a character trait or a tendency that is so embedded, so ingrained, we really can't do anything about it.

But that doesn't mean that *nothing* can be done about it. We'll discuss this more in the last chapter, when we talk about what to do with all those 'big problems' that we know a limited human being just can't do anything about.

For now, it's enough to have tried to dig out the truth, and to have the desire to improve things, however hard it appears to be.

Don't despair! There is an answer for everything, and a solution for every problem. We just need to know where to look for it.

Week 8 – Acceptance

This week, we're going to look at one of the most important components of feeling truly happy with ourselves, and with our life: acceptance.

For as long as we don't accept ourselves, and our circumstances, exactly how they are – with all their faults and flaws – we simply can't be happy.

Why?

Because a person who doesn't accept themselves for who and what they are is never living in the moment. They are always waiting for tomorrow to come, when they will be thin, or clever, or married, or 'successful', or popular, or rich.

And when a person is always focussed on 'tomorrow', they miss out on all the tremendous good they still have today.

Let's take a classic example of someone who is overweight. They may be 30 lbs heavier than they want to be today. Ok, it's not healthy to be so overweight. Ok, they'd feel much better, emotionally and physically, if they stopped carrying around all that excess weight.

But unless that person can accept themselves as they are, and accept that even when they are 'fat', they still have worth, and that they still have so much good in them, and that their life is still amazing - even if they diet down to the 'right size', they will still be miserable.

They tried to lose weight, and it worked – they've achieved their target weight or dress size. They're happy for a day or two, and showing off to everyone about how 'great' they did to lose all that weight.

But if they couldn't accept themselves, and love themselves, when they were overweight, they are already fretting about what will be if (when…) they fall off their diet and pile the pounds back on.

People who focus exclusively on 'tomorrow' are always miserable, because even if 'tomorrow' turns out to be great, they are still always worrying about what the next 'tomorrow' will bring.

That's why our Happy Workshop Principle number 3 is:

Happy Workshop Principle 3:

Live in the moment. Don't worry about tomorrow until you are there.

People who don't live in the moment are full of anxiety, dissatisfaction, sadness and depression.

So now, let's ask ourselves a question:

What is stopping us from living 'in the moment'?

The answer, at least for most of us, is that: *we don't like our current reality; we are dissatisfied with our lives; and we can't accept that this imperfect life, and imperfect 'us' is exactly how it's meant to be.*

Accept what we can't change

There's a famous dictum that says what you can't accept, you have to change, and what you can't change, you have to accept.

It sounds good in theory, but the trouble comes when you feel you really can't accept something, and you still can't change it.

- I can't accept that I have a 'terminal' disease
- I can't accept that my child is disabled
- I can't accept that the bank is foreclosing on my house
- I can't accept that I don't have the money to go on holiday this year
- I can't accept that someone I loved very much died

We humans like to think that we control everything.

We don't.

We have ridiculously high expectations that modern medicine can cure every disease (it can't…); or that we'll always be able to solve any problem we have by throwing more money at it (we can't…); or that people life forever (they don't).

All these things sound nice, and sound 'ideal' – but they simply don't reflect reality.

The reality is that there are some things that we can do something about; and there are many, many things that are simply beyond us. If we expect to be able to change those things, we are setting ourselves up with a massive expectation that simply can't be met – and we all know what happens when we have an expectation that can't be met: we get **really miserable.**

Happy Workshop Principle 5:

One of the key reasons we feel sad and depressed is because we have expectations that aren't being met.

Happy Workshop Principle 6:

The fewer expectations we have, the happier we will be.

Accepting ourselves

But how can we accept ourselves, when we know we still have a whole bunch of flaws, faults and failures? How can we accept our circumstances, when they are difficult, and painful, and horrible?

It's a good question – but it's the wrong one.

The right question is: Can I really **do** anything about it?

If the answer is 'yes' – then we have an obligation to try to do whatever is required.

(The answer is nearly always 'yes, I can do something about it' when it comes to changing ourselves, and our bad character traits and nasty habits. That's what the Happy Workshop is all about.)

But if the answer is 'no', we have to accept our lot, and do our best to be happy with it.

If this sounds unfair or harsh, what's the alternative?

We are all different

Accepting ourselves, other people, and our circumstances brings us a lot of inner peace.

A key part of accepting ourselves and others is to remember:

- We are all different
- We are all unique
- We are all on our own tailor-made path, and what is 'right' for one person is not 'right' for another
- We all require a different set of circumstances to fulfil our potential in life

In the following exercise, we're going to find out what we're finding it hard to accept about ourselves, and then, we're going to see which of those things we're stuck with, and which we can actually do something about.
I
Exercise 21 – What can I really change?

Make a list of the things that you dislike about yourself; divide the list into two parts. Call one part: 'externals', and list all the physical aspects, to do with your appearance, or external achievements and circumstances, that you aren't happy with.

Call the second part 'internals', and list the 'spiritual' and emotional aspects of your life that you aren't happy about, that have to do with how you act, behave or think.

Once you're done, take a different coloured pen and put an asterisk (*) next to the things you believe you can really change.

Example

Under 'externals', I wrote:

- Too short
- Mousy hair
- Unfit
- Bad dress sense
- Can't cook
- Nasty neighbours
- Hate my job

Under 'internals', I wrote:

- Worry a lot
- Get stressed easily
- Very sensitive
- Shy
- Not very sociable
- Hard on myself, and on other people
- Lack self-confidence

When I go back over my list, I asterisk the following:

'Externals'

- Too short
- Mousy hair*
- Unfit*
- Bad dress sense
- Can't cook*

- Nasty neighbours*
- Hate my job*

'Internals'

- Worry a lot*
- Get stressed easily*
- Very sensitive
- Shy
- Not very sociable
- Hard on myself, and on other people*
- Lack self-confidence*
- Not very competitive

Now, I have to work on accepting all the things that don't have an asterisk, and stop wasting my energy on wishing they were different.

Do a new list with all your asterisked items.

Next to each item, write down a couple of different ideas of what you could start to do to change them, or improve them.

If the effort and expense involved in changing 'mousy hair' starts to feel like it's too much – it probably is too much. Consider moving 'mousy hair' off your action list, and stick it back on the list of things that you just have to accept. Don't waste any more time or energy fretting about it.

If you hate your job – look for a different one! If you don't want to do that, then you have to accept that even though you hate your job, you actually prefer to stay in it than go through all the hassle of looking for a new one. Once you're honest – you *can* do something about it, but really you don't want to –

accepting that 'truth' will also help you to feel a whole lot happier about the situation.

Accepting our difficult circumstances

We don't choose our circumstances. If we did, we certainly wouldn't choose a whole bunch of things that are happening in our lives right now. Most of the time, we **can't change** the things that are really hard for us. The only thing we can change is **how we react to them.**

Happy Workshop Principle 13:

Often, we can't change our difficult or painful circumstances. But we can always change how we react to them.

Every day is full of potentially difficult 'life changing' challenges:

- Your boss calls you into his office, and tells you they are laying people off – and you're one of them...

- You get a phone call from the doctor's surgery, telling you that they've found something 'nasty' on the latest scan...

- The person you hoped you were going to marry dumps you...

- You fall out with a very close friend, and find out they've been bad-mouthing you to everyone...

- Your kid gets suspended from school for attacking a teacher…

- Your close relative has a massive heart attack, and unexpectedly drops dead…

The 'worst' has happened, and there is nothing you can do about it.

How are you going to react?

Your mindset is going to make all the difference between bouncing back, and growing and improving from these challenges, and getting flattened.

The people who accept their circumstances can work through them, make whatever changes they need to, and go on to live even happier, more fulfilled, content, calm lives.

The people who can't, get bitter, angry and vengeful. They use a lot of medication, drugs and alcohol to blot out reality. They start up witch-hunts, and vendettas, trying to find 'who to blame' and to make them pay. They obsess over their loss, or their pain, or the 'bad hand' they got dealt by 'life' – and they turn into morose, miserable, depressed, angry, nasty people who nobody wants to be around.

If you can't accept the 'hard' or painful things that you can't change or do anything about, that could be you.

Accepting the unacceptable

So now, the question of all questions: how can we accept something that we simply can't accept? How can we be happy about things that are genuinely making us miserable?

You'll find the only real, lasting answer is in the last chapter, but this week, we're going to work on accepting the unacceptable by practically applying our Happy Workshop Principles.

Let's take a typical 'bad' situation that happens to most people at some point in their lives, and work through it.

"I lost my job in a terrible job market"

You were working for the same company for 14 years. They liked you, and you liked them. You were happy with your colleagues, enjoyed your work, and built your whole life around the 'routine' you developed in the workplace.

Now, the whole company is shutting down, and you're out of a job. You still have mortgage payments, one kid in colleague and other financial responsibilities. You have some savings to see you through a few months – but then what?

It's a very tough job market, with people being laid off all over the place. You know it's going to be very hard for a 40-something guy like you to find anything, and you've already resigned yourself to working much harder, probably for less pay.

You're very worried about the future, and finding it hard to sleep. The stress is also creating an 'atmosphere' in the home, and that tension is starting to affect your family.

(Before you read the Happy Workshop....)

How can you accept these circumstances? How can you be 'happy' about them?

Let's work it through:

Happy Workshop Principle 1:

Don't make your happiness depend on an external change in your circumstances. What if it never changes?
Instead, be happy with whatever your circumstances are, and look for all the good you already have in your life, however small.

Ok, you lost your job, but you have some savings, or a loan from a family member, to tide you through and give you a bit of a breathing space, while you're looking for another one.

You can still meet your basic financial commitments, have a roof over your head and put food on the table, even though the 'luxuries' like eating out and having a vacation will have to go on ice for a while.

You're good at what you do and were well-liked in the workplace, and you have a lot of useful experience and a bunch of good references.

Your wife is being very supportive, and is helping you to track down new job leads, and proof-reading your covering letters and CVs. The daughter in college has already offered to try and look for part-time work to help offset the cost of her tuition, and your son was disappointed, but reacted very stoically when you told him you won't be able to get him a second-hand car now, when he turns 17.

You never realized how strong they were, how much they cared about you, how much you actually like and respect your family members, or how grateful you are to have them in your life.

You have a lot of time on your hands, and it's starting to drive you mad that you are spending so much time in the house.

You know that this could really make you miserable, so you decide to make a list of all the things you wanted to do, 'when you had more time':

- Fix up the house
- Start jogging – build up to a half marathon in the Spring
- Write a book
- Take an online tutorial to learn to play the guitar
- Upload all your music on to your iPod
- Go camping Upstate with your son for a few days

You know you need a routine to function, and to get you out of bed, so one of the first things you do is set out a schedule for each day. You pencil in time to job hunt and send out CVs; time to be out of the house jogging, walking, working out, gardening; time to be doing DIY, and time to learn guitar.

Regardless of your how your jobsearch goes, each day is now full of things that you enjoy, and you still have a sense of purpose. You are also counting your blessings that you have a loving family to stand by you, and savings, or a loan, to help cushion the financial blow until you find your feet again.

Happy Workshop Principle 2:

Real happy doesn't come from externals. Real happy stays with you, even when things aren't going your way.

Apart from the fact that you don't have any money coming in, life is actually pretty good.

Now that you are exercising every day, and have cut back on the restaurant food, you are feeling fitter and healthier than you have done for years, and you have a lot more energy.

Most of the time, you feel quite positive and upbeat – and you're amazed to realize that apart from the cash flow issue, you're actually feeling pretty happy. (Even though you don't have a job!)

When you do have a bad day, or moment, you check back through your 'good things' notebook, and realize that you still have so many things to be grateful for – and that gives you an instant 'pick me up', and chases away your looming bad mood.

But you are still stressing over the money, and that makes the atmosphere quite tense at home, particularly when a bill lands on the doormat that needs to be paid.

How to deal with the money stresses? Let's go to principle number 3.

Happy Workshop Principle 3:

Live in the moment. Don't worry about tomorrow until you are there.

Up to this point in your life, you've always had food to eat and a roof over your head. Even if you've gone through some hard experiences, you can see that sooner or later, everything turned around for the best – as long as you kept a positive frame of mind.

There is no reason to think that things aren't going to work out this time, too.

But let's say, they don't. Let's say, you don't find a job for months and months. Can you **do** anything to change it?

Happy Workshop Principle 4:

We can't control everything that happens to us, and neither can anyone else.

Aren't you already sending out all the CVs you can, and scanning the want ads, working your LinkedIn contacts, and signing up to online jobsearch engines?

What else can you really do?

If you think it's 'all down to you' – you are going to go mad, spending every spare moment surfing the net and firing off cover letters, and you'll let go of all the other good in your life – like the time to exercise, the time to read, the time to learn a new skill, or the time to really get to know your family.

There is a time for everything, and as long as you are making a reasonable effort, you don't have to worry that 'you aren't doing enough'. That's a shortcut to feeling increasingly frustrated, anxious and depressed.

Something else to consider: people who are giving off 'desperate' or 'stressed' vibes don't make a good impression when they're job-hunting. The more you worry about tomorrow, the more uptight you'll get, and the harder it will be to find a job.

Relax! Don't worry about tomorrow until it comes. Think through all the things you worried about in the past – how many of the 'bad' things ever actually happened?

Even if the 'worst' does happen, there is **always** some hidden good, even in the hardest situations. If you keep a positive mindset, you'll come through it a stronger, happier, calmer person, and you'll see why it all had to happen that way.

Happy Workshop Principle 5:

One of the key reasons we feel sad and depressed is because we have expectations that aren't being met.

If it's been a few weeks, and nothing is happening, you may start to succumb to 'poor me' syndrome. Poor me! I lost my job… Poor me! I have so many bills I can't pay… Poor me! I feel like a failure…Poor me! I can't afford to keep up my gym membership, get my hair done or buy a new pair of sneakers…

You now have the chance to see how many of those things that you tell yourself you 'need', you really don't.

Do you really 'need' a Starbucks coffee for $4 every day?

Do you really 'need' another pair of shoes?

Do you really 'need' an iPad upgrade?

Why?

You're also being given a golden opportunity to really get to know yourself, and to recognize a lot of the 'hidden' expectations, that are affecting your decisions, moods, actions and desires, without you even realizing it.

Let's say that you got into the habit of buying your kids something new every few days, regardless of whether they actually needed it. Now that you can't do that anymore, you may get some amazing insights into whether that was really a 'good' thing, or not.

- Were the presents to make you feel better that you weren't spending enough quality time with them?

- Were they a way of saying 'sorry' for things you've done or are doing that are really not acceptable?

- Were you trying to buy their respect, or love?

- What were you expecting from them, as 'payback' for the gifts?

Again, these are tough questions. But if you've been given the chance to re-examine some of your most fundamental 'expectations' – grab it, and don't be scared about where it takes you.

If you learn the lesson that your kid would prefer a heart-to-heart chat, or to kick a ball around with you, any time over getting a pricey new watch – that lesson by itself could be a key reason why you had to go through this whole experience.

Happy Workshop Principle 6:

The fewer expectations we have, the happier we will be.

It's great to have a goal to aim for; it's a huge mistake to have a fixed expectation that 'I will find another job within three months'.

Set your goal – finding another job asap – but keep any other expectation to a minimum. If three months comes and goes, and you still don't have work, you just set yourself up for a massive emotional nose-dive. Once you're down, it's so much harder to pull yourself back up.

Happy Workshop Principle 7:

We will only find genuine happiness once we figure out why we're REALLY unhappy.

If you've spent all your life being valued, and valuing yourself, by the money you make, or the 'career' you have, or the things that you buy – being out of work for an extended period of time can really shake you to the core.

It can bring everything into question: will people still want to talk to me, if I'm poor and unemployed? Will they still love me? Will I love myself?

Anything that's 'real' doesn't depend on external circumstances. If a person loves you, they love you regardless of your bank account. If they walk when the money disappears – it means they never *really* loved you in the first place.

This principle also applies to our relationship with ourselves: when I was making a six figure salary, I didn't think too much about my character development, and what I was actually 'doing' in the world.

I work! I earn a lot of money! What else is there?

Once 'money' and 'career' disappears, that's when we can really see what's underneath: who are we, really?

Are we selfish, or do we try to do kindnesses for others? Are we patient, or anger-prone? Forgiving, or vengeful? Nice, or nasty?

Once the money and status has gone, you'll see your true nature reflected in the people you hang out with. If they drop you like a hot-cake – it's a sign that apart from what you could buy for them or do for them, they actually didn't like you very much.

If they hang around, and try to help you and support you – it's a sign that while the 'easy life' was nice, you have a lot more going for you and your relationships than just your bank account.

This might be a time of very painful realizations. But remember, once you work out what's **really** making you miserable, you're more than half way to making the changes you need to make to be **really** happy.

Happy Workshop Principle 8:

When you're dealing with other people you can either choose to be 'right' – and to stand on principle – or you can choose to be 'happy'. But you normally can't choose both.

If you get rejected from your ideal job – don't fight it. Don't get upset. Don't make a big deal, and try to force people to reconsider their decision.

All these things take an awful lot of energy, and never, ever create anything 'positive'. Even if you persuaded them to change their mind, do you really want to be in a new job where no-one actually wanted to hire you? What stress! What pressure to perform, and to prove yourself!

If you didn't get the job, accept the decision calmly, and put your energies into continuing your jobsearch.

All that happened is that it wasn't the right job for you – however it looked at the time. It doesn't matter how perfectly-qualified you are, how well the interview went, how much you wanted it – if the job still went to the boss's completely unqualified little sister, that's how it's meant to be.

Happy Workshop Principle 9:

The issues that really get under our skin with other people is the stuff that we ourselves need to work on.

The recruiter promised to get back to us four days' ago, and we're still waiting. They're avoiding our phone calls, not responding to our emails.

We're starting to get really angry, paranoid and upset at their disgusting behaviour.

This is not the way to treat people!

Until...until...we remember that we promised to sit and go through the maths homework with our middle schooler ages ago, and we still haven't made the time to do it.

Until...until...we remember that we haven't returned that call from a friend who wants to borrow our power drill, and we keep telling the kids, or the wife, to tell them we're out, when they call.

Until...until...we realize that every time we think we're going to have an awkward or difficult conversation with someone, we keep putting it off until we get backed into a corner, and can't avoid it anymore. And then, boy, do we get mad at the person who's doing that to us.

Stop bothering the recruiter. Go away, and work on your own 'avoidance' issues, and once you do, the recruiter will start calling you...

Happy Workshop Principle 10:

If movies, Facebook and newspapers are making you miserable, then take a break and either reduce them significantly, or cut them out altogether.

Every time you pick up the newspaper, you read about more jobs being laid off in your industry, or in your area. You get a big lump in your throat, and start to feel really, really demoralized. How are you ever going to find a job, in this terrible market?

Stop reading the news. Look at the jobsearch section, and ignore the rest.

If you catch yourself feeling bad, or down, after you've looked at something, or read something, don't keep repeating the experience.

We are all individuals, we all have our own tailor-made path in life. Just because the latest economic forecast is terrible, that doesn't mean you won't get a job. Believe in yourself, and stop rating your chances according to the latest 'statistics'.

Even if it looks bleak, there are always jobs and opportunities available for people with a positive, upbeat mindset and the right attitude.

Happy Workshop Principle 11:

The more kindnesses we do for others, the more kindness and goodness we'll recognize in the world, and the happier we'll feel.

The first week I was out of work, I took a garbage bag and cleaned up my street. Since then, I've had a few conversations with some of the neighbours I've never spoken to in my life, who noticed what I was doing.

The second week, I arranged to take an elderly, house-bound relative out for the day – something we'd been talking about for months. She had a great time, and sent me a card a few days' later telling me how much she'd enjoyed it.

The third week, I went to the supermarket and bought everything I'd need to cook a great (but cheap...) meal for my spouse. I realized that even though I'm not contributing to the household budget at the moment, I can still show her I care in other ways. She was in a great mood, by the end of the meal.

The fourth week, my brother called to tell me that if there was anything he could do for me, I only had to ask. I'm not at that stage yet, but it was really good to know that he cares enough to see how I'm doing, and to make the offer.

Every kindness I do for others creates a 'virtuous circle' for me. I feel good, they feel good, and then I take that 'good vibe' with me into my jobsearch, my interviews, and hopefully, very quickly, into the new work place.

Happy Workshop Principle 12:

Instead of pointlessly beating ourselves up about our mistakes and failures, we need to 'solve the mystery' and do some honest introspection to find out what's really going on, why, and what we can do about it.

You've sent off hundreds of CVs; you've had tens of interviews – but still, no-one is offering you a job.

You could blame your CV, the job market, the 'sexist' or 'racist' or 'whatever-ist' interviewers; the bad reference you believe your last boss is giving you – or, you could sit down, and take some time to work out what's really going on here.

After 14 years in the same job, do you actually still want to be doing it, or are you ready for a change? Are you looking for work in the same field because you like it, or because it seems like the 'easy' option?

Is it time to consider a change of career? A change of direction? A move away? What dreams did you put on hold, because they were too scary to think about while you had a steady job?

Now that the job's gone, what other changes could you make to improve your quality of life? Were you really happy working 18 hour days, and never seeing your family?

Do you want your weekend back? Are you sick of the blackberry running your life, and coming out with you everywhere you go? Is it time to be your own boss?

If things aren't 'getting there' relatively quickly and easily, it's usually because we are trying to push on a closed door.

Look around for the door that's already wide open!

It could well be that you aren't getting the jobs you are going for, because deep-down, you don't really want them. Once you work out what's really going on, you'll have a much better idea of what you really want, and what you can and should do about it.

Happy Workshop Principle 13:

Often, we can't change our difficult or painful circumstances. But we can always change how we react to them.

We've come full circle.

No-one wants to be out of work, especially for an extended period of time. But by following the Happy Workshop principles, the person in our example:

- Stayed productive, and filled his day with useful activities
- Stayed positive, even when his jobsearch wasn't going very well
- Managed the stress over the money much better, and didn't make a bad situation worse by causing unnecessary or unbearable tension in the home
- Realized he is much more than his job; that his family and friends really care for him; and he really cares for them, and would like to have a better relationship with them
- Got to know himself, his family, and what really makes him happy
- Realized life is too short to spend all that time, miserable, in a job he was only doing for the money
- Decided to follow his dream, and to set up his own business

Things could have been so different.

As the jobsearch progressed, he could have got more and more stressed and worried, and less and less pleasant to be around.

The tension at home could have peaked until his wife had enough of his bad moods, temper tantrums and angry rants, and told him she wanted a divorce.

His feelings of being a 'loser' could have multiplied, and his one scotch a night could have gone up to eight, in an attempt to 'take his mind off' all of his problems.

Other friends and family members could also have had enough of being around a tense, angry person who kept ranting on about the boss who laid him off, leaving him even more lonely and isolated.

The jobsearch would stall; despair and depression would set in – and the situation would continue to spiral from bad to worse, until someone had mercy on him and gave him a copy of the Happy Workshop to read...

Exercise 22: The painful things I need to accept

Write down up to 10 'circumstantial' things that are upsetting you, or paining you. It could be illnesses, financial problems, family issues, things that happened in the past, things that are happening now, 'big' problems, or small irritations.

Look at the list of 'big ten' issues or upsets, and put an asterisk (*) against those you can actually do something about.

Now, write down everything you asterisked on a separate piece of paper called 'things I can do something about', and brainstorm to come up with solutions or answers.

Sometimes, we find a genuine solution to our problem or issue, but we aren't interested in it, maybe because it seems too hard, or the solution requires us to try to change ourselves, our habits or our lifestyle.

If you have items that fit into this 'middle category', make a note of them. At some point, you may decide that the big changes they require you to make are worth it.

Next, make a separate list of the things that you really and truly can't do anything about. Those things you have to try to accept.

Of course, you can always keep fighting, and keep complaining – that's your free choice. But unless you do your best to accept these things, and make the best of the situation, you'll be carrying around a lot of sadness, heaviness, and negative emotions for the rest of your life.

If accepting these painful things seems too hard at the moment, go back a step, and focus on accepting the idea, at least in principle, that accepting your painful circumstances will eventually take away most of the pain and suffering associated with them.

Even if the circumstance continues, it will no longer hurt you as much, or cause you as much suffering.

And that's surely something worth striving for.

Simple habits that keep us happy

In this chapter, we're going to sum everything up that we've learned together over the course of the Happy Workshop.

If you've been putting some effort into doing the exercises, being honest, and asking yourself the hard questions that we usually all like to try and avoid, you should already be noticing some tremendous differences in your life, your attitude, and your relationships.

The more you can internalize the Happy Workshop principles and ideas, the happier you'll be.

Let's start with a quick recap of why we get miserable:

We get miserable because:

➢ **We have bloated expectations**

- We expect too much and constantly get disappointed (both with ourselves, and others)
- We continually beat ourselves up for our 'mistakes', instead of doing some honest introspection to see what we can learn or change

➢ **We make unrealistic judgement calls about other people**

- We expect them to be perfect
- We assume that other people are 100% in control of themselves, 100% of the time
- We forget that everyone is different: what I find easy, other people find very hard, and vice-versa;

what I find obvious is 'hidden' to other people, and vice-versa

> **We take so much of the good in our lives for granted**

  - We chase after 'big' ticket items and luxuries, but forget that it's a gift every time we even wake up in the morning

> **We think we control everything, and that everything is down to us**

  - We don't accept our own faults and flaws, and we get hyper-defensive if anyone else notices them
  - We don't accept that other people find it as hard to work on their faults and flaws as we do
  - We get bitter about our painful circumstances and experiences, and let that pain consume all the good we still have in our lives, instead of accepting it, and trying to grow from it

Rabbi Nachman of Breslev tells a story about a 'sophisticated' man and a 'simple' man that sums up a lot of what we've been learning together in the Happy Workshop.

You can read a full translation of the story into English for yourself at www.azamra.org/essential/sophist.html but the gist is that there are two men, one clever, and one simple.

The very clever, very talented one goes off to seek his fortune away from home, while the simple one stays in the place where he grew up, and becomes a bad shoemaker.

Throughout the story, the clever, very talented one flits from job to job, getting more famous and more rich – and more miserable. The simple one gets married and barely subsists on his income, but he's always amazingly happy.

The simple one eventually gets a big break, and hits the big time. But his success doesn't go to his head, or turn him into a selfish, spoiled 'celebrity', because he learned when he was down-and-out that real happiness, real value, real worth, doesn't come from externals.

The clever one never learned this – and ends up wasting his life, his potential and his talents having pointless 'philosophical' debates with people, and trying to show them just how clever he is.

What we can learn from the story

The two characters in the story are basically a blue print for how to live a happy life, or how to be completely miserable.

The 'clever' habits that make people miserable

Miserable people:

-   Are very arrogant. They believe that they are the centre of the universe, and that everyone else 'owes them' something

-   Are very ungrateful, and take all their blessings in life for granted

-   Have very high expectations, and are constantly dissatisfied

-   Always worry about 'tomorrow', instead of living in the moment

- Sacrifice everything else in their life to achieve 'financial security'

- Are always trying to impress other people with their superiority (intellect, ability, wealth, achievements, connections, education etc)

- Are always worrying about what other people think of them (everything is done with an eye on the 'crowd')

- Excuse their bad behaviour and mistakes with rationalisations and justifications

- Never say sorry, or admit that they made a mistake

- Are very selfish, and only think about themselves

- Don't think other people are important, and are particularly dismissive about other people's feelings

- Think they are 'special' and exceptions should be made for them (instead of realizing that we are all unique, and that each person has their own good points, abilities, challenges and tasks in the world.)

- Are very superficial, and mock the idea that there might be a 'deeper meaning to life'

- Spend their whole life competing with others

- Don't know what they are here for

Confessions of a 'Clever-clogs'

The first time I read the story about the Sophisticate and the Simple Man was about five years' ago, and a very big, very painful light-bulb went off in my head.

Rebbe Nachman was writing about me!

I rarely stayed in a job more than a year; I was always looking for something 'new' somewhere else; I also picked things up very quickly and got bored of them very quickly.

I was convinced that my intelligence and education would get me places – and that I was so clever I 'deserved' great jobs with lots of money and respect

I was always competing with everyone else, at work and socially, and playing the ranking game.

I was terribly miserable, and trying to keep busy all the time (particularly with work).

I was constantly hoping the new dress, or the new bit of furniture, or the new 'experience' would fill the 'gap' – but it didn't for more than 2 minutes, and then the whole process would start over again.

I was searching for meaning in my life, and looking everywhere except the place where I eventually found it.

I was the clever-clogs!!!

And I was terribly depressed and miserable.

Until I found Rabbi Nachman, and his teachings.

So now, let's look at the habits that Rabbi Nachman says will keep us happy

Simple habits that keep people happy

Happy people:

- Don't complain

- Act in a moral way; they do kindnesses for other people, admit to their own mistakes and try to fix any problems that they created

- Don't compare themselves to anyone else

- Are very humble

- Are grateful for all their blessings

- Try to see all the good they still have in their lives, even if they are going through a bad patch

- Have patience

- Don't beat themselves up over their failures, and don't get big-headed over their successes

- Believe there is a 'higher purpose' to life

- Are full of real joy, that doesn't depend on their external circumstances

You're not there yet? You're still full of complaints, and dissatisfaction, and competition and victory-seeking? You're still trying to out-earn your neighbour and out-perform your work colleague? You're still telling yourself that everything bad that happens to you must be your fault, or someone else's fault? That you don't deserve all your bad breaks? That life's not fair?

Join the club.

It's very, very hard to break all those 'clever' habits of miserable people, because our whole society is built on them.

I've been trying to live the Happy Workshop principles for five years already, and I still have times when I catch myself in 'clever' mode (usually five seconds before I start to feel really down…)

Be kind to yourself. Have patience. Understand that these attitudes and habits have built up over many years, and it's going to take more than a few days or even a few weeks to unpick them all.

Most of all, keep a positive mind-set. How we believe it is, is how it really will be. If we think something is terrible, and there's no hope and it's the worst thing in the world – it will be.

If, on the other hand, we believe that's there's always hope; that there's always good, and that even if something is terribly broken, it can still be fixed, and made even better than new – then *that* will be our reality.

This applies to our circumstances, to our efforts at self-improvement, and also, to our relationships.

Keep looking for the good, for the break-through, and sooner or later, you'll find it.

Happy Workshop Principle 14:

We create our own reality. If we believe something is good, ultimately, it will be. If we believe something is 'bad' – then that's the reality we'll be stuck with.

Exercise 23 – Clever characteristics

Think of a circumstance or situation that you found extremely challenging from the last month or so. Write it down on a piece of paper, and try to identify what 'clever' characteristics were at play.

Were you:

- Trying to compete with someone else?
- Thinking about how you would look to other people?
- Feeling superior or inferior?
- Trying to force the issue?
- Thinking you deserve better, or different?
- Beating yourself up? (What if... If only.... Why didn't I....)
- Unable to recognize or admit that you'd made a mistake?
- Only thinking about yourself, and what you wanted?

Once you've identified the 'clever' habits that helped to create the circumstance or situation, go back to the situation, and try to work it through with a more 'simple' mindset.

How would things have been different if:

- You had more patience?
- You hadn't blamed yourself, or other people?
- You'd acted with more humility?
- You stopped competing?
- You thought more about the other person's point of view?
- You were more grateful?
- You were more accepting of yours (and other people's) limitations?
- You weren't trying to show off, or look good?
- You said sorry?

How could cultivating more 'simple' habits have helped you to create a more positive reality, or outcome?

The real solution to every problem

A lot of people get very turned off by the whole idea of 'God' so I've left that concept until the end of the book.

If you want to skip this chapter, you can. The rest of the book still contains some great advice for living a happier, more fulfilled life, and if most people lived by the Happy Workshop principles alone, they'd probably be incredibly happy nearly all of the time.

But there are some situations, some hurts, some problems, that no amount of self-help books, or counselling, or distractions can help you with.

That's where God comes in.

God can do anything.

You're still struggling to quit smoking, or to keep a lid on your nasty temper?

God can help you to do that.

You're still grieving over the child you lost, the love-of-your-life who dumped you, the horrible diagnosis, the missed investment opportunity-of-a-lifetime?

God can heal that pain.

You're still having terrible, 'dark' days when your head is full of horrible, destructive thoughts? You're still not the spouse you wanted to be, the parent you wanted to be, the human being you wanted to be? You can't count how many times you've tried to change, or measure just how badly you really want to improve – but you're still stuck, and you can't see how it will ever be different?

<u>God can change it. God can change you – in the blink of an eye.</u>

God can do anything.

But first, we have to believe in Him.

I don't know which version of 'God' you were brought up with, or told about, or maybe ran away from, but God is full of kindness and compassion for His creations. He's full of good ideas for how to solve our problems and heal our hurts.

He knows that we aren't angels, that we aren't – and can't be – 100% perfect, 100% all the time.

He made us!

He just wants us to try to live a moral life; to try to do as many kindnesses for other people as we can; to build the world around us; to own up when we do make mistakes and try to 'fix' what we broke - and to talk to Him as much as possible.

This book is not the time or the place to go into these ideas in any detail. But if you're stuck in a dark place, or stuck with an unsolvable problem, or stuck with a massive bundle of guilt, just remember: *God can do anything*. We just have to ask Him to help.

If you want to read more about developing a healthy, positive, 'real' relationship with God, you'll find some recommendations for some great books in my reading list, at the back of the book.

Even when we are failing, even when we are doing a terrible job, even when we fall down again and again – God always wants us to get up, and get closer to Him.

Wherever we are, we can turn around and call out to God – and He'll answer us, and bring us closer.

And getting closer to God is the whole point of why we are down here in the first place.

Regardless of your circumstances, or your issues, if you try to see God behind it all, and try to be happy with your lot, *you will get closer to God.*

And the closer you get to God, the happier your life will be.

BONUS: QUICK GUIDE TO HOW TO DO MIND MAPS

Introduction

Many of the exercises in this book are a form of 'mind map' exercise. Mind maps are a deceptively easy, simple way of being able to tap into the subconscious mind, to see what we're really thinking and believing about a whole bunch of things.

They're also an incredibly versatile tool, and can be applied to almost anything you care to mention, from organising a party to figuring out some really deep stuff about your psyche.

I've put the following quick guide together as a bonus for 'Happy Workshop' readers, to help you master this incredibly useful tool, and start applying it to your own life and circumstances.

What are mind-maps?

I've been doing mind-maps for more than 15 years, and I've done hundreds of them, both for myself, and also as a mind-map facilitator for other people. I first found out about mind-maps when a business consultant friend of mine told me about how useful they could be for organising the new PR business I was trying to set up at the time.

That first mind-map blew me away. It took all the stuff that was blocking up my head, and got it out of my brain, and down onto paper, in a way that made it so much easier for me to figure out what needed to happen, how, when, and why.

This sort of **organisational mindmap** is invaluable for when you have a big project to do, and you need to set down clear processes, goals and priorities. You'll find detailed instructions walking you through this type of mind-map a little later on.

Deeper applications for mind-maps

The beauty of mind-maps is that you can apply the same basic mind-mapping tools to almost every area of your life - even very deep emotional stuff. Mind-maps can also help you to find answers to big questions like: 'what do I want to really do with my life?' Or: 'what's going to really make me happy?' Or: 'what should my priorities in life really be?'

Questions like this can often seem so overwhelming and confusing, not least because so much seems to hanging on the final decision. Doing a mind-map can give you instant clarity about what's really going on in a particular area or your life; or how you might want a particular area of your life to improve or change.

You'll get detailed destructions for how do this sort of deeper sort of mind-map a little later on, in 'Big Interview' mind-map example.

These sort of mind-maps can save you thousands of bucks in therapy bills; give you instant clarity and direction; and you can apply them to literally anything you want.

Another advantage to mind-maps is that once you learn the basic skills, you can also start showing your friends and families how to do them, too. But if you start facilitating other people's mind-maps, you have to remember one very important rule (especially if you're doing a mind-map where you have a personal interest vested in the outcome):

Each person's mind-map has to reflect their own ideas, opinions, preferences and desires - not yours!

Facilitate all you want, make suggestions, set a direction - but encourage the person you're helping to express what they truly think and feel, otherwise the mind-map won't reflect their reality, and will be a waste of time.

Example: The High School mind-map

Let's say you want to help your kid to decide what high school, college, or course to go to. As the parent, you probably have your own preferences, but in order for a mind-mapping exercise to work, you'll have to put all your ideas aside, and give your child the space to see what THEY really want.

This is often very hard for a parent to do, so if you can't approach the mind-map in a neutral way, either don't do, or get someone else to facilitate it.

But if you're happy to help your child to discover what they actually want and prefer, then a mind-map can be an amazing way of enabling your teen to find their own clarity.

In this particular example, the teen in question got some very useful insight into herself as a result of doing a mind-map, and realized she actually didn't want the 'top' school she'd applied to. As a result, she decided to go to a school that was more laid-back, academically, but otherwise a much better fit for her in every other way.

The Basic Rules of Successful Mind-Mapping

The following rules apply to every mind-map you do, regardless of whether it's simple, complicated, deep, practical, emotional, or whatever.

Rule 1: Get G-d involved

All your help, all your insights, are going to come down the pipe from God. Time and time again, God has given me flashes of inspiration via mind-mapping that have been the 'missing piece' of the puzzle. Even if you don't know what you're doing, or you just feel completely stuck in a situation, decision, or problem, get G-d involved and He'll open up all sorts of ideas and possibilities for you.

Rule 2: Be honest

This is more important when you're doing deeper stuff, but even for the most simple, practical mind-maps, be as honest as you can. For example, if you know you don't want to spend more than half an hour cleaning up every day, don't set goals or targets that would require 2 solid hours of cleaning a day. Doing a mind-map based on incorrect or faulty assumptions and information might sound good, but it won't help you to actually change your reality.

Rule 3: Don't censor yourself

This is often connected to Rule 2, but is coming from the opposite direction. If you find yourself phrasing anything with a 'should' when you're doing your mind-map, stop and challenge the assumption: is it SHOULD or is it WANT? I SHOULD change jobs, or I WANT to change jobs?

SHOULD usually shows up when we're trying to people please, or put other people's ideas and preferences ahead of our own.

Rule 4: You can't do this wrong

There is no such thing as a 'wrong' mind-map. Even if it doesn't turn out the way you planned; even if you can't seem to write what you wanted, or make sense of what's going on, each and every single mind-map contains myriad clues about what's going on in that area of your life.

EG: if you can't even begin to write down what needs to be arranged and taken care of before you can start to get your new business idea off the ground, that by itself is showing you that you're completely overwhelmed by the whole idea. If that happens, take a step back, and instead of doing a 'Next Steps For My New Business' mind-map, maybe do a 'why is this overwhelming me so much?' mind-map instead.

(And then book a long weekend away and a massage…)

Rule 5: No two mind-maps are the same

Mind-maps, as the name suggests, are a map of your mind. We're all different, unique, individuals, which means that everyone's mind-map - even for the same subject - will look and be completely different. Don't compare your mind-map to anyone else's. Your particular style and flavour of mind-map is reflecting your beliefs and personality back at, in precisely the way you need, in order for you to do or learn something, or make the change that might be required.

Rule 6: Judge yourself favorably

If a mind-map is really doing its job, it's going to show you some very honest things about yourself. Not all of your mind-map insights are going to earn you 'feel good' brownie points, and some of them may even be pretty disconcerting and uncomfortable.

The evil inclination just loves making people feel bad because they aren't perfect. Whatever secret ikky thing you discover about yourself via doing your mind-map, on no account should you start beating yourself up about it. On the contrary!

When you attain this sort of clarity about yourself, it makes God really happy. Whatever issues, character flaws or nasty traits you discover, there's a very good reason why you have it, you just don't know what it is yet. But God does. He's judging every single thing you do favorably, and He wants you to do that, too, and to be kind to yourself, and to not beat yourself up under any circumstances.

Rule 7: Keep an open mind

To put it another way: don't shoot your arrow, and then paint the target around it. The whole mind-mapping process is about discovering what's really going on inside of you, and in your mind, at the deepest levels. Let the process unfold, and give yourself the space you need to learn some new things about yourself and your true outlook and perspective.

Rule 8: Translate your mind-map into real time

At the end of each mind-map, write down a clear list of action points, targets, goals and deadlines, to help move your clarity from 'theory' to 'practise'. (The following exercises will give you some concrete ideas for how to actually do this.)

Rule 9: Pray on it

If anything awkward, difficult, overwhelming, shocking, surprising or challenging reveals itself in your mind-map, don't panic - just pray on it. If you suddenly realise that you actually really hate your job, or that a close family member's behaviour is distressing you far more than you ever realised, don't have a heart-attack. Take a deep breath, make space for G-d, and ask Him to show you how to resolve the particular problem, difficulty or issue. Then just wait for the amazing idea, or insight, or solution to pop into your head, or your life.

Rule 10: Write spontaneously

Don't over-think your mind-map. If when you're doing a mind-map, you're finding it very hard going, or not coming at all, it's usually because you're blocking your own answers and truths in some way, or feeling blocked by something or someone else. If you write something down on your mind-map and then cross it out - challenge yourself. Why are you changing your mind? Who or what are you scared of, if you keep your first answer? Why do you think it's wrong?

Whenever you catch a 'conflict' in your mind-map - it's a big red sign that you just hit an area where you need to do some more digging, to see what's really going on. Ask G-d for clarity, and keep probing. You'll get some answers, and when you do, you'll see how your insights into yourself, your self-confidence, and your perceptions start to change and improve.

That's it!

Exercise 1: The preparing a birthday party mind-map

The *thought* of preparing for a birthday party, event (or whatever other big project you're working on, or avoiding, or procrastinating about) is usually far more overwhelming than the actual doing of it. Like every project, once you set down the parameters of what's actually required, it stops being so scary and anxiety-provoking, and it shrinks down into something manageable, and even, maybe enjoyable.

So let's shrink this birthday party sucker down into something doable, and start breathing again.

STEP 1:
Take your piece of paper (larger is usually better, at least A3 size)

STEP 2:
Get God involved in the process, in whatever way you're comfortable with. Some people like to write 'with God's help' in the top corner of their mind-map; others will just send out a quick thought that God should help them to get the answers they need; still others will put a few coins in their charity box. Whatever works for you is fine.

STEP 3:
Next, put 'preparing the birthday party' or 'my birthday party prep' or something like that, in a circle in the middle of the paper, and put a circle round it. Remember this is a blue-print for an organisation mind-map, and you can use the steps described here for any organisation task or job, from cleaning out your closets; to sorting out all your financial papers; or rearranging your whole human resources department.

STEP 4:
You can do the next bit however you like:

- break it down by tasks
- break it down by categories
- break it down by priorities

Break the project's different components down into smaller elements in whichever way you want, just make sure it reflects your actual style. For example, if you want to break 'birthday party prep' down into tasks, the next stage of your mind-map will look like this:

The idea is to arrange the related tasks or elements around your central mind-map theme, the same way spokes are around the central hub of the wheel. Each idea is connected to the main idea, but it's going off into its own sphere, and will have its own separate considerations and elements.

You can use different colour pens for each separate task or category, to really start bringing it to life.

Step 5: The next step is to see if you need to breakdown your main categories further, into smaller sub-categories. For example, 'Catering' is one of the things you have to organise for the birthday party. But that's not the whole story.

So under 'Catering', you're going to either list all the things related to that particular task, or you're going to make 'Catering' the hub of a separate mind-map spoke.

Whichever way you pick, the idea is have all the different elements of 'Catering' clearly set out, vis:

- Ask friends for catering recommendations
- Get quotes from caterers
- Check with the birthday girl or guy what food preferences they might have
- Set catering budget
- Check caterer's availability

STEP 5: Start prioritising

Now, you need to start prioritising the list you just made under 'Catering'. Again, you can do this in a few different ways: some people may want to prioritise it in terms of importance; others, in term of what needs to be done first; others, in terms of how much time each particular thing is going to take, or how much money it's going to cost.

How you prioritise your mind-maps is going to depend on the goals you want to achieve.

In the 'Birthday Party' example, you might choose to prioritise like this:

1) Check with the birthday girl or guy what food preferences they have
2) Set catering budget
3) Ask friends for catering recommendations
4) Get quotes from caterers
5) Check caterer's availability

Often when you start to prioritise, that's when you'll start to get some very helpful insights. In this example, it could be that you'll be working on the catering, when you'll actually realise that you need to know where you're holding the party, before you can actually make that decision.

Are you going for a marquee on the lawn, or renting out a hall, or doing something more original and 'out there', like holding your party by the beach in a forest? Is there going to be an onsite kitchen, or does everything have to be pre-prepared?

Other insights will also flash up, like you need to think about if the weather is going to be hot or cold; or how many people you'd like to invite. If it's 14, you can afford to splash out a bit more on the food. If it's 400 - cheap and cheerful is the name of the game.

All of these insights start to coalesce into a big picture, that will actually guide you towards the right decisions, and the next steps you need to take.

Whatever organisation project you're working on, make sure that:

1) You're BEING HONEST about how you actually work, and your preferences, and your limitations;

2) Forget about 'SHOULD', and

3) Keep your priorities realistic.

STEP 6: Draw your conclusions

This is where the real mind-map magic starts to work.

Maybe, you'll look at your 'to do' list for the birthday party, and you'll realise that you have loads to do, and not enough time to get it all done. You've just uncovered something profoundly useful, namely that you need some help in order to pull the project off.

Now, you can start to think about who might be willing to help you, and what things you might be able to delegate to them.

Or maybe, you'll realise that the birthday party you were planning out in your head is far beyond your budget or time constraints. If that's the case, you need to figure out a different sort of birthday party: maybe, it needs to be on a smaller scale? Or maybe, the catering could be less fancy? Or maybe, you decide it's better to scrap the idea all together, and spend the money taking the birthday guy or girl skiing for the weekend instead...

At this stage of the mind-mapping process, you should have enough information set out to help you to start drawing some conclusions about what needs to happen, when, and how.

STEP 7: Set yourself goals / action points

The last step of the mind-mapping process is to turn your insights into a solid plan of action. Based on what you now know are your priorities, you can start to create a list of action points, and where appropriate, you can attach deadlines to them.

Some action points for the 'Birthday Preparation' mind-map could include:

- Set a budget for the party by the end of the week.
- Find a caterer by the end of next week.
- Get the invitations printed for 2 weeks' time; send them out in 3 weeks' time

And so on, and so forth.

Remember that the same basic recipe that you've learned in this example can be applied to any other organisational issue, problem or decision.

In the next example, you'll learn how you can apply the same basic mind-mapping principles to matters of the mind and spirit.

Deeper mind-maps

OK, now we've seen how to apply mind-mapping easily to de-cluttering our brains and our homes from all the stuff we need to do, organise, clean, sort out.

You can use mind-maps any time you feel overwhelmed, and need to prioritise what to do first, or next. But you can also use mind-maps for more deeper things, and that's what we're going to try to do now.

The second mind-map we're going to do is called:

The Big Interview

At some point or other, you'll probably have to participate in some sort of big interview, or meeting. It could be for a new job, a new school, a blind date, a meeting with your kids' teacher, a talk with your bank manager to try and get a mortgage.

Many people find these types of interviews and meetings nerve-wracking, and they can bring up a lot of difficult emotions and surprising reactions. If you do a mind-map beforehand, it can help you to work through how you want the interview to go, and also help us you to identify any possible problems or big issues, and work on them, before you even get there.

This is an example of how a mind-map can help you to catch your deep-seated emotions, and deal with your subconscious responses, BEFORE they could trip you up on the day itself.

Exercise 2: The Big Interview Mind-map

STEP 1:
Take your sheet of paper, and put the words 'The Big Interview' (or big meeting) in the middle of the page, in a circle.

STEP 2:
Get God involved in whichever way you're comfortable with, as outlined in Step 2 of the first example, above.

STEP 3:
Now, you're going to free-associate. Without over-thinking (or thinking too much at all…) just write down whatever comes to mind, as you think about the upcoming interview or meeting. Even if it sounds a bit 'weird', unrelated, or 'out there', write it down. These seemingly extraneous pieces of information are often hiding some very deep issues and ideas.

STEP 4:
Now, take each of the categories you've written down around your 'hub', and give them a rank out of 10. 1 is 'not at all distressing, disturbing or stressful', and 10 is 'maximally disturbing, distressing or stressful'.

Do this spontaneously; your unconscious mind will write down your truthful response, if you get yourself out of the way enough to let it.

STEP 5:
Now, try to associate a feeling, or emotion with each think you've written down. For example, if you wrote down:

Don't know what to wear - what emotion or feeling is that actually conveying? Are you scared of looking stupid? Or doing something wrong? Or being judged harshly?

Go through each thing, and try to catch the underlying emotion, feeling or concern. Write it down next to it.

STEP 6: Start to prioritise
Mind-maps are as much an art as a science, especially when dealing with emotional states. Now, you're looking for a theme or a priority that's weaving its way through your reaction to the big meeting or interview.

Is there a particular feeling or issue that keeps coming up, repeatedly, in different places? Like worried you'll look stupid? Or, scared you'll do something wrong and mess it up? Or, scared of 'failing', in some way?

If that turns into a dead end for you, try another tack: go back to your ranking system, and see which issue, or issues, carry the most weight for you. If anything's got a high number beside it, pay it some attention, and look to see what's the related emotion or underlying fear?

That's your priority.

STEP 7: Draw your conclusions
Again, this mind-map example is just a guide, and shouldn't be taken as THE blueprint of how to do these types of mind-maps. Be guided by your intuition, and your soul.

The conclusions in these types of mind-maps tend to split into categories:

1) Practical and functional
2) Insightful and transformative

For example, if you're super-worried about turning up late to your big meeting, then there are certainly practical, functional conclusions you can draw about the need to leave in plenty of time; or taking the bus instead of driving, so you don't need to waste time finding a parking spot etc.

These types of conclusions deal with the superficial concern on the day, but don't address the underlying emotional issue.

An insightful and transformative conclusion is something that doesn't just tackle the symptom of the problem, but gets to work on the core.

Examples could include:

- Making a commitment to trace the anxiety about being late back to its root.
- Using an energy psychology tool like Emotional Freedom Technique, or the Tapas Acupressure Technique (TAT) to start defusing the excessive emotional charge and worry associated with being late.
- Getting God involved, and working on your emuna, (belief or faith), so that it's easier for you to accept that God's running the world, and you don't have to start beating yourself up or blaming yourself for being late, especially if you did everything you could to be on time.

You get the idea.

STEP 8: Set yourself goals / action points

Again, this last step can be split into practical, functional action points that deal with tangible issues and problems; and more long-term goals or action points, that start to address the underlying emotions.

To continue with our 'scared to be late' example, the practical action points could include:

- Drive the route at the time you need to be at the meeting, but a day or two before, in order to get an accurate idea of how long the journey will actually take, and to scope out the parking facilities.
- Check the bus schedule.
- Make the necessary babysitting or car pool arrangements, etc to enable you to leave at the right time, on the day of your interview.

The long-term goals or action points will vary from person to person, so the following is just to give you a flavour of the sorts of things they might include:

- Set a deadline for yourself to do a mind-map solely on the issue of being scared to be late.
- Take the free, JEMI 'Talk to God and Fix Your Health' online course, to get more of a feel of where the fear of being late is really coming from.
- Commit to talking to God for a minute every day about dissolving your irrational fear of being late.
- Do a TAT session, solely on the issue of being petrified of being late.

Whatever type of action points you come up with, pin yourself down! Don't make wishy-washy statements, instead make serious commitments, attach a deadline to them, and then do your best to achieve them.

If you don't manage to achieve all of your action points or goals, don't get discouraged. Go and talk to God about what's really going on, do another mind-map, talk things over with a close friend that you trust, and you'll see that one way or another, things will start to move again.

RECAP: The basic rules of successful mind-mapping

The following rules apply to every mind-map you do, regardless of whether it's simple, complicated, deep, practical, emotional, or whatever.

Rule 1: Get G-d involved in the process
Rule 2: Be honest
Rule 3: Don't censor yourself
Rule 4: You can't do this wrong
Rule 5: No 2 mind-maps are the same
Rule 6: Judge yourself favorably
Rule 7: Keep an open mind
Rule 8: Translate your mind-map into real time
Rule 9: Pray on it
Rule 10: Write spontaneously

Recommended reading

Websites:

www.emunaroma.com
Author Rivka Levy's personal blog, talking about modern life, God, husbands, kids, health, books and of course, chocolate.

www.jemi.website
The official website of the Jewish Emotional Health Institute (JEMI). Find out how to apply God-based holistic healing to your health and wellbeing.

www.talktogod.today
Blog and website about how talking to God can help you to fix everything from your health, to your bank balance, to your marriage, and a few other billion things besides.

Books:

By Shalom Arush:

The Universal Garden of Emuna - how to see God in every aspect of your life
The Garden of Education - how to raise your kids in a spiritually healthy way

168

OTHER BOOKS BY THE MATRONITA PRESS:

Talk to God and Fix Your Health
The real reasons why we get sick, and how to stay healthy. A detailed but easy to read explanation of why good health needs to take body, mind and soul into account. Includes an introduction to meridians, exercises and appendices full of practical advice showing readers how to identify the root of their health issues, and what steps to take to resolve them.

The How, What and Why of Talking to God
In introductory Pocket Guide to why regularly talking to God can make the single biggest difference to your health, happiness and success in life. The guide explains what talking to God is all about, and gives practical, detailed instructions for how to start talking to God.

A Spiritual Blueprint for Understanding and Overcoming Personality Disorders
An holistic look at what's causing the modern epidemic of Personality Disorders, and how to tackle the problem at every level of body, mind and soul.

How Your Emotions are Making You Sick
A detailed Pocket Guide to which emotions are linked to which Energy Meridians, and how blockages or issues in a particular meridian can lead to particular physical problems.

Causes and Cures of Depression
Details the spiritual, emotional and physical reasons causes of depression, and gives lots of practical tips for how you can make your depressions a thing of the past.

For more details of these and other books, please visit us at:
www.matronitapress.com

Thanks for reading this book!

If you enjoyed it, please take a moment to give it an online review at any of the following sites:

www.amazon.com
www.goodreads.com
www.booktalk.org
www.shelfari.com
www.bookpage.com
www.librarything.com